Fairies, gnomes & trolls

create a fantasy world
in polymer clay

Fairies, gnomes & trolls

create a fantasy world in polymer clay

maureen carlson

NORTH LIGHT BOOKS
Cincinnati, Ohio
www.artistsnetwork.com

10 09 08 07   5 4 3

Distributed in Canada by Fraser Direct
100 Armstrong Avenue
Georgetown, ON, Canada L7G 5S4
Tel: (905) 877-4411

Distributed in the U.K. and Europe
by David & Charles
Brunel House, Newton Abbot,
Devon, TQ12 4PU, England
Tel: (+44) 1626 323200,
Fax: (+44) 1626 323319
Email: postmaster@davidandcharles.co.uk

Distributed in Australia by Capricorn Link
P.O. Box 704, S. Windsor,
NSW 2756 Australia
Tel: (02) 4577-3555

Library of Congress Cataloging-in-Publication Data
Carlson, Maureen
  Fairies, gnomes, and trolls : create a fantasy world in
polymer clay / Maureen Carlson.
     p. cm.
  Includes index.
  ISBN-13: 978-1-58180-820-9 (alk. paper)
  ISBN-10: 1-58180-820-8
  1. Polymer clay craft. 2. Fairies in art. I. Title.
  TT297.C2685 2006
  731.4'2--dc22
                          2006012509
Editor: David Oeters
Design and layout: Amy Wilkin/Dragonfly Graphics L.L.C.
Cover Designer: Karla Baker
Production Coordinator: Greg Nock
Photographers: Maureen Carlson, Christine Polomsky and Al Parrish
Photo Stylist: Jan Nickum

fw
F+W PUBLICATIONS, INC.

metric conversion chart

to convert	to	multiply by
Inches	Centimeters	2.54
Centimeters	Inches	0.4
Feet	Centimeters	30.5
Centimeters	Feet	0.03
Yards	Meters	0.9
Meters	Yards	1.1
Sq. Inches	Sq. Centimeters	6.45
Sq. Centimeters	Sq. Inches	0.16
Sq. Feet	Sq. Meters	0.09
Sq. Meters	Sq. Feet	10.8
Sq. Yards	Sq. Meters	0.8
Sq. Meters	Sq. Yards	1.2
Pounds	Kilograms	0.45
Kilograms	Pounds	2.2
Ounces	Grams	28.4
Grams	Ounces	0.04

about the author

*t*his book brings Maureen Carlson's work with polymer clay full circle, as it was a gnome that started her adventure with clay. It began in 1978 on a dreary, rainy weekend during an arts and crafts show at Stan Hywet Hall in Akron, Ohio. Since she and her fellow artists had time on their hands, she began creating clay mushrooms, which at that time embellished her calligraphed plaques. The artist next to her looked over at the mushrooms and said some words that changed her life forever (though she didn't know it at the time). "You need to make some gnomes to go with those mushrooms. Tomorrow I'll bring you my book of gnomes." And so began a journey that continues to this day.

Maureen, like the characters in this book, is a wearer of hats and a believer in masks. Like all of us, she plays many roles, including those of teacher, author, retreat facilitator, Storyclay Teller, wife to Dan, mother to Jenelle and Renee, and grandmother to Ian and Gideon. These days, she does most of her work at Maureen Carlson's Center for Creative Arts, in Jordan, Minnesota. You can find out more about her at www.maureencarlson.com. This is her fifth book with North Light Books.

dedication

i dedicate this book to Larry Randen, who first introduced me to the works of Joseph Campbell and his book, *The Power of Myth*. It was Larry's belief in the power of stories, and in my ability to tell them, that gave me the nudge I needed to take myself seriously. And what I have learned is that "serious" can be so much fun!

acknowledgments

*t*here were a lot of people involved in making this book happen, from the attendants at the gas station who were still there late at night when I was just heading home at the end of a long day, to Marie Robling, my yoga instructor, who helped me remember that it's all part of the flow. Then there's my family: the Carlsons, Boyers, Pecks and Tarrants, who keep me connected to what is real and true. Thank you to my students, who have always taught me more than I've taught them. Thank you to Val Daniels, whose hands are in the how-to shots, and to Lolly Gosewisch, for bringing some sanity and order to my Center for Creative Arts.

Of course, there would be no book at all if it weren't for the people at North Light Books, who have beautifully put all of this together. Until you work on a book, you never understand how important an editor is to its success. Thank you, David Oeters. Also, be sure and look at the names listed at the bottom of the previous page to see who was responsible for the beautiful photos and design. They are the ones who really turn my work into magic.

table of contents

a *Journey* with the *Faerie Folk*

Something magical happens when you open the cover of a book, especially one such as this, whose subject is the Faerie Folk and how to make them. Opening the cover is like answering an invitation to explore a whole new world. Of course, the choice is always yours. Once inside its pages, you could choose to close it up again and go your way, but, if you linger awhile, chances are you'll never be the same.

Flip through the pages of this book and you'll meet some of the residents of the Faerie World. There are characters such as Broogen Bogge, the slow-moving Rock Troll, or Marvin, the Trickster Elf. Take a look at some of the easy-to-follow directions, and read a few of the stories. Does it feel like a place where you belong? Do you wonder if, perhaps, you could become a sculptor of clay characters and a teller of tales? What may have seemed only the subject of dreams could suddenly become a real possibility. Linger long enough and the result just might be a whole world of little clay people, inspired by the book, but created by you.

In this book we'll be using the ancient word, Faerie, to refer to all of the inhabitants of this enchanted world, whether they be elves, gnomes, trolls, sprites or fairies. The word fairy, spelled with an *ai* in the middle and a *y* at the end, will be used only for those who were chosen to be born with wings.

Two of the characters, Woodpecker Pete (page 81) and AnnaBelle Mae (page 82), will be your sculpting and storytelling guides throughout the book. Woodpecker Pete, who is an excellent woodcarver and sculptor himself, will provide helpful tips for working with clay. He will also be encouraging you to think beyond the ideas presented in the main projects so that you might be inspired to come up with your own variations. AnnaBelle Mae, who is a storyteller, will be sharing tales about each character. She'll also be suggesting ways to tell your own stories through each of your creations. After all, everyone has a story, whether that someone is you or a figure made from clay. Telling stories about the characters makes them seem to come alive. Plus, knowing someone's story makes you more forgiving of his or her weaknesses, even if they are your own.

Maureen Carlson

an introduction to polymer clay

the magic of clay

Polymer clay is a magical material. All that you need in order to become a clay magician are a few packages of polymer clay, some simple tools, an oven and a willingness to begin. Add a few simple tricks, a dose of imagination and a pinch of practice, and you can turn polymer clay into almost anything.

It's also the perfect material for both beginning and experienced sculptors, since polymer clay works equally well in simple or exquisitely detailed designs. Since it doesn't air-dry, you can play, create, smash and start over, but once it is baked, your work will be permanent.

When purchasing clay for the projects in this book, I recommend that you use one of the stronger clays, such as FIMO Classic or FIMO Soft, Kato Polyclay or Premo! Sculpey. For more information on polymer clay, please consult the resource guide at the back of the book. Whatever clay you choose, you must knead it to warm it up before use. This is known as conditioning the clay.

polymer clay safety

Polymer clay has been tested safe for general use by the Art & Creative Materials Institute. It is a polyvinylchloride compound, which makes it a relative of everything from margarine containers to silk flowers. But it does require

certain safety considerations: Polymer clay should never be eaten or burned. These two rules are easy to follow if you remember these tips.
* Dedicate all of your polymer clay tools to craft use, and don't use them again for food.
* Thoroughly clean your hands, as well as all work surfaces, after using polymer clay.

uses for polymer clay

Polymer clay is extremely versatile and can be used for many applications. Because it is a plastic, water doesn't hurt it, so it is can be placed outdoors (however, the sun may damage and fade the color). Polymer clay placed in direct contact with soil may pick up stains.

Polymer clay is strong, but it's not unbreakable. For maximum strength, all parts of a project need to be very well-baked. If strength is required, consider adding a wire armature for both support and strength (see page 15 for more information on armatures).

mixing clay

Different polymer clay colors can be kneaded together and mixed to create new colors. As you are mixing colors, you may wish to write down the types of clay and how much of each you used. Bake a small test piece to see if heat

Polymer clay comes in a variety of colors and package sizes

Polymer clay garden art at Maureen Carlson's Center for Creative Arts

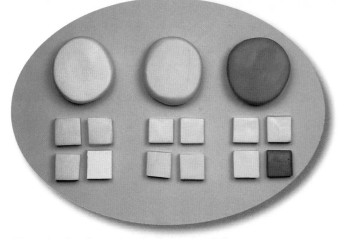
Three simple color recipes for flesh-colored clay

Propping will help keep your projects safe in the oven

changes the color. If you like the final result, then save that recipe in a file. Before many of the projects in this book you'll find the color recipes I used for that project.

While you can use any color for the flesh of your characters, here are three simple recipes, pictured above, for flesh color. The pale mix is three parts FIMO Classic #43 Flesh Pink mixed with one part FIMO Classic #0 White. The middle is FIMO Classic #43. The darker mix is three parts FIMO Classic #43 mixed with one part FIMO Soft #7 Caramel.

storing clay

Since polymer clay does not air dry, it can easily be stored for future use, but keep the clay away from intense heat, such as sun-lit windows or heating elements, until you are ready to bake or cure it. Store clay at average room temperature, preferably in plastic bags or covered containers to keep it clean.

baking clay

Polymer clay does emit some fumes while baking, which, over time, result in a buildup of oily residue along the sides of the oven. Since tests show occasional usage falls well within the safety guidelines, a home oven may be used for baking clay projects. however, to be on the safe side wipe out the oven after every use and don't bake clay at the same time that you are baking food. It might be helpful to bake in a dedicated covered roasting pan, which can be washed frequently and is used only for clay. If you frequently bake polymer clay, it is a good idea to purchase a clay-dedicated oven.

Temperature and baking-time guidelines for polymer clay are listed on the packages of clay. It's always a good idea to read and follow them. It's also critical that you use a separate oven thermometer for setting and testing your oven temperature. Many ovens just aren't accurate, which will result either in burnt or inadequately baked clay.

Polymer clay gets soft and weak when it gets hot, so it is a good idea to prop it every time it goes into the oven. Propping tools may be ceramic, metal, paper, foil or glass. Place a piece of baking parchment or a paper towel between the clay and hard surfaces so you aren't left with a shiny mark on the clay.

the sculptor's toolbox

basic tools

Kitchen-supply and hardware stores are some of the best sources for tools, but remember, tools used for clay should *only* be used for clay. I suggest you gather these basic tools and have them on hand before you start a project:

- *Oven:* A clay-dedicated toaster oven will work. Just make sure the projects you make will fit in it. My oven of choice is a large, portable convection oven that I use *only* for baking clay.
- *Oven thermometer:* An accurate oven thermometer is critical to the success of these projects.
- *Work surface:* A smooth, nonporous work surface such as glass, marble, waxed freezer paper or a plastic countertop works best.
- *Small knife:* This knife doesn't need to be sharp.
- *Polymer clay blade:* This is a sharp, thin blade, that is useful for cutting and trimming clay.
- *Needle tool:* A needle, or pin, tool that has a sharp point.
- *Knitting needles:* Knitting needles are larger than needle tools and have a blunt end. My favorite sizes are 3, 5 and 6.

- *Clay brush:* Stroke a small amount of clay into the bristles of a good-quality size 3 or 4 paintbrush to stiffen them. A clay brush can be used for smoothing clay.
- *Rolling tool:* Look for an acrylic clay roller or brayer.
- *Plastic drinking straws:* Plastic straws are excellent for making simple mouths and fingernails.
- *Baking pan:* A ceramic tile also makes an excellent baking surface.
- *Aluminum foil:* Foil is a necessary material for making armatures and is useful for baking clay.
- *Paper towels:* Use paper towels to add texture, clean up paint and prop characters in the oven.
- *Round-nosed pliers:* Use pliers to work with armatures and wire. Flat-nosed pliers and wire cutters are also useful.
- *Scissors:* A good pair of scissors is always handy.

other tools

You'll find a more complete listing of the tools you'll need before each project. Knowing how to get the most out of your polymer clay tools and supplies is the key to a successful project.

- *Pasta machine:* The pasta machine is a time- and muscle-saving device and is useful for making sheets of clay. Clay must be quite soft and about the thickness of a thin pancake to pass cleanly through the machine. Clay that is cold, stiff or too thick may crumble. Some people choose to use the pasta machine to condition clay, passing it through until the clay is soft and flexible.

- *Liquid clay:* Liquid polymer clay, such as Liquid Kato Polyclay, Liquid Sculpey and FIMO Liquid Polymer Clay, has a multitude of uses. In this book, it is used as a painting medium (for the Green Man, page 42) and as an adhesive (for Drey Van Elm, page 108, and Isa Rosalia, page 114). It can also be used as a softener by mixing it into stiff or crumbly clay. Some liquid polymer clays bake matte, and others bake to a semi-gloss finish. I like the matte finish, which is invisible once baked unless it is very thick, in which case it can leave a texture.

- *Adhesives:* Because polymer clay is a plastic, many glues do not adhere to it. Some even turn sticky, so test a glue well before applying it to your masterpiece. For bonding raw clay to baked clay, liquid polymer works quite well. To bond nonporous items, such as baked clay or wire, use a cyanoacrylate glue, also known as instant glue. To attach hair or fiber, use a flexible glue such as Beacon's Fabri-Tac.

- *Sealer:* Polymer clay doesn't need to be sealed; however, you may wish to seal the paint on the faces. Many sealers turn sticky after awhile when applied to polymer clay, so be very cautious about using a sealer that either you or someone you trust has not tested. I use a spray sealer, such as Duncan's Porcelain Ceramic Sealer or Super Matte Ceramic Sealer if I want a matte surface on my characters. For shiny parts, such as eyes, I use one of the clay supplier's gloss sealers, such as Eberhard Faber's FIMO Gloss Lacquer.

- *Food processor:* Before using polymer clay, it needs to be conditioned. Not all packages of polymer clay will feel the same. The consistency of polymer clay varies depending on many factors. Because of this, it is very useful to have a quick method for conditioning it in order to make it soft and pliable. Softeners, such

A pasta machine

A food processor

as Polyform Company's Clay Softener or Clay Diluent, Eberhard Faber's Mix Quick or one of the liquid polymer clay products, can also be added to clay in a clay-dedicated food processor and blended into a cottage-cheese like consistency, then mixed by hand.

notes from Woodpecker Pete

If you need a tool of a specific shape or size, make it from polymer clay, then bake it. Clay also makes a great handle for small needles. To help secure the needle into the clay, wrap thread or wire through and then around the eye of the needle before adding the clay.

a closer look at characters

making a plan

Now that you have an understanding of both polymer clay and the basic tools that you need to work with clay, let's talk a bit about actually making characters.

The first step in creating a clay character is to have a plan. Without a plan, what was intended to be a fairy might turn into a troll! And one gnome could grow to twice the size of another. This isn't a problem if you are making only one character, but if you intend to make a community that will be displayed together, then their size and shape needs to relate to the others. This relationship is called proportion.

Woodpecker Pete the elf and a gnome

proportion

Take a look at Woodpecker Pete, an elf (page 81), and a gnome (page 74). They are basically the same height, yet they appear very different. The critical difference is their proportion.

Look at the size of each character's head in relationship to its body. Woodpecker Pete, an elf, is $4^{1}/_{3}$ heads tall and his head is very narrow. The gnome is $3^{1}/_{2}$ heads tall and his head is rounder. These differences may seem minor, but even subtle variations such as these change the overall shape and appearance of a character. To me, the elf's smaller head in relationship to his total height makes him appear to be wiry and quick, while the larger head and wider body of the gnome make him seem a bit more earth-bound. This is proportion at work.

I have designed the proportions of each of the characters in this book to reflect my particular image of each race of Faeries. So, for example, Isa Rosalia, the Garden Fairy (page 115), is almost $7^{1}/_{2}$ heads tall. Her smaller, narrower head in relationship to her height makes her seem older as well as more delicate.

hands, feet, arms and legs

I also considered proportion when making the arms and legs for each of the fantasy characters. The length of the arms and legs, and the size of the hands and feet, varies greatly depending on both the age and the type of Faerie Folk being made.

In general, the fairies and some of the elves in this book have average human proportions, while those of the gnomes and trolls are more exaggerated. This exaggeration is one of the clues that tell us we are dealing with characters from the world of the Faerie Folk. For example, most adult humans have hands that are two-thirds to three-fourths the height of the head, but those of Drey Van Elm (page 108) are longer and wider to reflect his mystery and power.

Please feel free to change the proportions for each of the characters in this book in order to reflect your own vision of the Faerie world.

Proportion helps make characters unique

An armature is like a skeleton

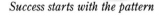

Success starts with the pattern

armatures

When you look at the characters in this book, you don't see their armatures, but every character has one. An armature is what holds them together and makes them strong. It also fills up space and saves on the amount of clay being used, so that the clay bakes more evenly.

Characters that are less than 1" (3cm) thick, such as Ophelia Lilliana (page 32) are often made of solid clay with just a wire to support the head. Larger characters, such as Magical Mischievous Marvin (page 102), have an aluminum foil core. No wire is needed to support Marvin's arms or legs, but a looped wire head armature helps control his size and also stabilizes his neck. Characters with large, flat surfaces, such as the Green Man (page 42) or Theodore Funguy (page 54), have an armature made from expandable wire mesh.

If a character is standing, such as Drey Van Elm (page 108), but does not have visible legs, an all-foil armature may be used. A standing character with legs, such as Isa Rosalia (page 114), will need a wire armature to support the legs. My favorite armature wires for characters less than 10" (25cm) tall are brass rods. They are rigid and strong, yet bendable.

Don't hurry too quickly through the making of the armatures, as the shape and proportions of the armature will affect the appearance of the completed character. I encourage you to read and follow the armature measurements that are given at the beginning of each project.

using a pattern

For some characters, such as Sweet William (page 88) or Isa Rosalia (page 114), proportion is critical to the success of the project. For these characters, patterns are included on pages 122-125. Using the pattern and armature will help maintain the proportion as you sculpt. Lay the wires on top of the pattern, then bend them, using pliers to follow the angles.

Once the individual pieces are cut, lay the wires on top of the outline drawing. Connect the pieces of the armature by wrapping it with a 28-gauge or smaller wire. Be sure that the assembled pieces fit within the drawing. Be sure to leave enough space so that a layer of clay $1/8$" to $1/4$" (3mm to 6mm) thick can be added to the outside of the armature.

sculpting basics for everyone

Making clay characters is really quite simple, but what makes a piece special, and what makes you a master craftsman, is the ability to add subtle details. Here are a few of my favorite techniques, which, once mastered, will turn a plain ball of clay into any character that your mind can imagine. Learning these basic shapes and techniques will help you as you work through the projects in this book.

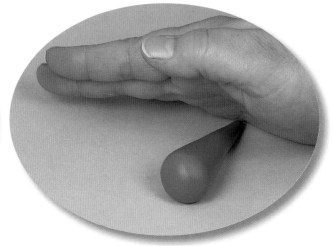

the ball

Place the clay in your palm and roll it in your hand to create a ball of clay. Make sure there are no wrinkles or lumps in the ball. The ball is the quickest shape to make, and rolling a ball is the easiest way to get the clay smooth.

the teardrop

To create a teardrop from a ball of clay, place your hand on one side of the ball, then roll it against a hard surface. One side of the ball will lengthen until the shape becomes a teardrop.

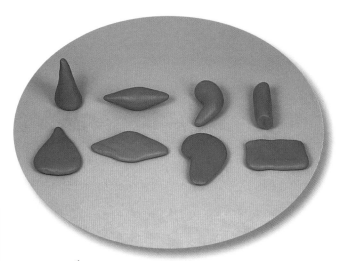

notes from Woodpecker Pete

The consistency of polymer clay varies and can affect how you work with it. The temperature and humidity of the room and your hands can also affect the clay. You may need to make the clay stiffer or softer as you work. See the package of clay for more information on this process.

more shapes

Stand the teardrop upright and press down on the wide end to create a cone. Roll your hand against the wide end of the teardrop to create a football shape. Bend the narrow end of the teardrop over and it becomes a comma or a lopsided teardrop. Roll the teardrop into a ball, then roll it back and forth on your work surface to create a rope. Each of these shapes can also be flattened for use in creating the characters and faces in this book.

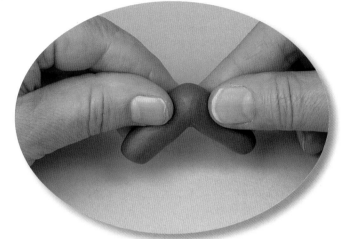

creating sharp bends

A quick turn will make sharp bends in a piece of clay. Hold the clay with both hands so that your fingers are on the sides of the clay. Bend the clay gently so that the sides stay round. Now, with your fingers still on the side, gently push the clay toward a place halfway between your two hands. The sides should still be round, not flat, but with a sharp bend in the center. Smooth any rough spots with your finger.

hollowing out clay

To hollow out the center of a piece of clay, press a rounded tool, such as a dowel or a sturdy paintbrush handle, against the clay. Hold the clay still with one hand and press down on the tool with your other hand. Roll the tool, not the clay, back and forth until the sides of the clay become thinner. Shift the clay so that the tool touches another section and repeat. Continue until all the sides are even.

notes from Woodpecker Pete

Remember, because this is clay, it is easy to smash a piece and start over. It's better to do it earlier in a project, when making the basic shapes, than later!

creating curves

I call this technique "the drumstick roll," because it reminds me of the curve in a chicken drumstick. To make a piece of clay bulge and give the appearance of muscles or flowing curves, make the basic shape for the clay, then hold it with two fingers, just below where you want it to bulge, and roll the clay back and forth gently. To make the bulge recede again, repeat the rolling process just above the bulge.

bringing characters to life

All of the figures in this book are made by combining basic clay shapes. The key to making a character who seems real, as if there were actual flesh and blood under those clothes or behind the skin, is to blend and shape the clay so that nearly every surface is rounded or curved. This gives the clay figure the appearance of a living, breathing creature.

shaping clay

Try to shape the clay as you smooth it. Here, the top side of the nose was blended into the forehead as the bridge was narrowed and the eye socket and brow bone were created. If you are using stiff clay, you may have to distress the edge first by scraping it with a knitting needle, then blending the jagged edge into a smooth one.

creating a curved surface

In this example, which is the back side of a pair of pants, a curved surface was made by first pressing in a deep line with a knitting needle. Next the needle was gently rolled first toward the indentation, then away, to gradually round the clay into a curve. On larger pieces you can also use your finger to smooth and shape the clay. Use gentle, repetitive movements so as not to move the clay too much at one time.

notes from Woodpecker Pete

It can be tough to get clay really smooth. There are liquids that will help with the final smoothing. Some clays, such as Super Sculpey, may be smoothed with water, though don't mix water into the clay because it may create imperfections that are visible under the clay surface. Other clays smooth well with denatured alcohol applied with either a brush or your finger. My favorite smoothing medium is Sculpey's Clay Softener (also called Clay Diluent), which I apply with a brush. It dissolves the clay and creates a blending paste. Do this as a last step, as it does make the clay sticky. Add too much and the surface will become rough.

working with faces

Give expression to a face by rounding the clay edges and changing the depth of the lines around the mouth and eyes. Do this either by adding clay along the line, such as when you add clay for the cheek, or by deepening a line, as when you press in crow's feet around the eyes. To soften the line, use a round tool to softly roll towards the line, then away. Keep the surface curved. For more information on working with the face, see page 22.

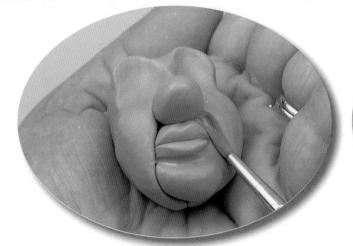

using a brush

In those places where you can't use your finger to smooth and blend the clay, use a clay brush. It works as both a smoothing and sculpting tool. Choose a good-quality brush that does not have loose hairs. Brush in the direction that you want the clay to move. The secret is repetitive brushing. See page 12 for more information on the clay brush.

working with fabric

You don't actually have to sculpt clothing for your characters. You can lay out a thin sheet of clay, just as if it were fabric, and cut pattern pieces. Then "stitch" them together by overlapping on the seam lines and smoothing. Be sure the clay is at least $1/16"$ to $1/8"$ (2mm to 3mm) thick and that the finished piece is well-baked. Otherwise the thin edges might break. For pattern ideas, use actual clothing pattern packets and copy the shapes that are used to make real clothing.

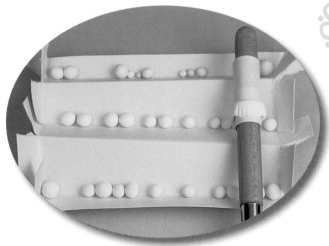

notes from Woodpecker Pete

When adding raw clay to baked clay, such as when working with prebaked elements like eyeballs, use your fingers or a rounded tool to smooth the raw clay onto the baked clay. Use the rounded tool to scrape off excess clay as you blend. Keep repeating this motion until the surface is as smooth, and the seam between raw and baked clay is as gradual, as you can make it. Then do a final smoothing, using either your fingers or a brush. In areas where the raw clay is attached but not blended, a little liquid polymer clay will act as an adhesive.

prebaking

Prebake some of the clay parts, such as eyeballs and teeth. Once baked, these pieces will retain their shape as you add, blend and smooth the clay around them. Characters may also be baked in stages. Bake carefully, as some brands of clay will scorch or darken with repeated baking. A foil tent over the character will help shield the delicate noses and ears from intense heat.

sculpting hands

Hands can be almost as expressive as faces. Once you understand the basic shape of hands, experiment with positioning them so that your clay characters seem to "talk" with their hands.

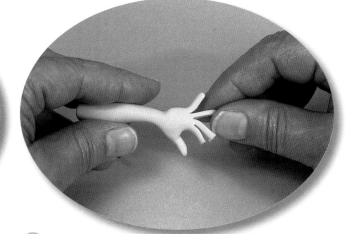

1 To make a hand, start with a smooth ball of clay. Roll the ball into a rope that is as thick as the arm. Make the arm longer if you are making the hand and arm together. Do a drumstick roll at the wrist. Flatten the hand in a slope so that the finger area is thinner than the wrist. Cut out the extra clay from between the thumb and fingers. Use a round tool and your fingers to smooth the edges and stretch the thumb.

2 You can just leave the hand flat. But to make it look as if it can move, bend the thumb, as well as the clay on that side of the hand, over toward the little finger. Support the clay so as not to distort the rest of the hand. Or you can cut the fingers apart for more realistic hands. Trim the lengths of the fingers so that the little finger is the shortest. Separate the fingers and carefully pat and roll the ends until they are smooth. Use a brush to smooth any other areas.

3 If you decide to make nails, use very sharp scissors to cut out a nail-shaped protrusion on one end of a drinking straw. Keep the edges as smooth as possible. Press the tool first into the cuticle area, then rock it from side to side. On larger nails, also press the tool under the tip of the nail. Gently smooth the nail toward the tip to slightly flatten it.

4 To shape the palm, roll a knitting needle along the top of the wrist, then from the bend of the thumb toward the bottom middle of the palm. Use a smaller needle tool to add crease lines.

sculpting feet

Most of the characters in this book wear shoes, but you can easily
replace the shoes with bare feet.

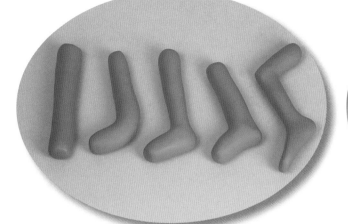

1 Roll a ball of clay into a rope that is as thick as the thickest part of the leg. Do a soft bend at the heel, keeping the sides round. Do a quick turn to make a defined heel. Flatten the foot so that it slopes from the ankle to the toes. Stretch the leg to smooth and refine the ankle. Cut the foot to the desired length. Make a knee, doing another quick turn and a drumstick roll (see Creating Curves on page 17) to give it shape.

2 Your characters can have a wide variety of feet. The differences between feet are mostly in the shape of the toes. Hollow out the top and a foot becomes a shoe. Cut lines for toes and leave the top solid and it becomes a bare foot.

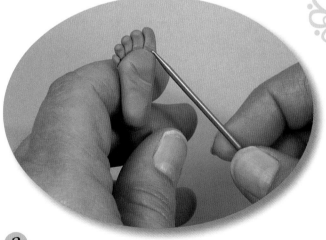

notes from Woodpecker Pete

*Polymer clay seems to pick up a million
little pieces of fiber, hair and fuzz. You
can eliminate some of the fuzz and dirt
by cleaning your hands frequently with a good, water-
less hand cleaner or a nonalcohol wipe. Keep your work
surface as clean as possible. Avoid wearing dark-colored
clothing or clothing that sheds.*

3 Give the bare foot an arch by pressing your thumb into the bottom of the foot on the side with the big toe. Use a needle tool to add wrinkles at the base of each toe and across the foot.

sculpting the face

The faces for most of the characters in this book were made by combining a few basic shapes. When you learn to see the basic shapes in a face, the process becomes much easier.

1 Decide on the size of the character's head, then make an armature for the head. Heads that are less than 1" (3cm) thick can be made from solid clay. For the pictured sample, foil was crumpled into an egg shape, then flattened on one side. Cover the armature with a sheet of clay ¼" (6mm) thick. Use a needle tool to draw facial features. Just a line drawing will do. Include the eyebrows, eyes, nose and mouth. You may also draw the chin and cheek lines.

2 Sculpt each of the facial features, using the following directions: *Forehead:* Roll a rope, then flatten it into a rectangle with indentations for the brow bones; *Nose:* Roll a teardrop, then press it into a triangular cone; *Cheeks:* Roll two flattened, lopsided teardrops; *Lips:* Roll two flattened, short cone triangles with one thicker edge; *Chin:* Roll a flattened, short cone triangle; *Ears:* Roll two flattened teardrops, with an indentation pressed into one side; *Eyelids:* Roll two flattened footballs; *Eyes:* Make two small, prebaked white clay balls.

3 Lay each shape on the clay head, following the lines you drew. Trim the pieces that are too big or overlap with a clay blade. You can begin to smooth the clay as soon as you add a piece, but don't complete any one section until all parts are added.

4 Use a needle tool to blend the seam lines. Use gentle pressure so as not to flatten the clay. Begin to shape the features as you blend. Use a sharp needle tool to separate the lips and clean clay out of the eyes.

5 To add character and expression to the face, deepen the lines around the mouth and eyes. Smooth and soften the lines by rolling a round tool into and then out of the indentations. Curve the ears so that they have more shape. You may want to refer to pictures of faces while sculpting. The only tools that I used to add these details were a knitting needle, a sharp needle tool, a clay brush and rubbing alcohol for the final smoothing. When finished, bake following the instructions on the package of clay.

6 Antiquing adds variations in the color, plus makes the lines more visible. Choose a shade of acrylic paint that is just slightly darker than the face. Apply a thin mix of water and paint, called a wash, using a firm brush. Wipe the paint away immediately with a paper towel. Use another brush to remove paint from the wrinkles and grooves. Use water to remove any excess paint.

7 Add blush to the cheeks, chin, nose and ears using coral or rose acrylic paint mixed with a small amount of matte gel medium. Pat the blush with your finger or a sponge to blend the edges. Use a brush to add tiny dots with brown paint in the areas that have blush. Before the paint dries, pat the dots with a moist finger to disperse the paint. For freckles, leave the dots visible.

8 Use a tiny brush to paint a colored iris. Imagine that it is a circle, with the top and bottom of the iris behind the lids. Let the paint dry between coats. Start with a darker color, then stroke a lighter color toward the center. To make a round pupil, dip the tip of a pointed brush into paint and carefully touch the center of the eye. Add a tiny white highlight to the line between the pupil and the iris. Use a nearly dry brush and a lifting stroke to add eyebrows and eyelashes.

notes from Woodpecker Pete

Be cautious if the baked clay face is rough, as rough spots will hold more paint. Don't worry if you make a mistake. Use water to quickly remove it before it dries. Sometimes rubbing alcohol will remove stubborn paint spots.

the World of the Faerie Folk

I believe this book can be read on many levels. It's a project manual that teaches you how to create clay characters, but it's also just plain fun to thumb through the pages and see the characters develop from mere lumps of clay. Gradually imagination creeps into the mix as you read the stories. Sometimes, you find yourself entering into the world of the Faerie Folk and adding your story to theirs. When this happens, it's evident that more is going on than just the creation of clay characters. To explain, let me tell you about my journey with the Faerie Folk.

My first efforts at creating with clay were little characters that I called Wee Folk. And take my word for it, they were very crude. But there was something magical about the process that kept me at it until I got better and learned more. It led to my business called Wee Folk Creations, then to the Minnesota Renaissance Festival and a booth beside the Hobbit Hole. Next, I began writing my first how-to booklets—on fantasy characters, of course. This led to the creation of a whole world of little people, called Pippsywoggins.

The story might have ended there if it weren't for a serendipitous meeting in the mid-1980s with Larry Randen, a believer in the power of myth and stories. He looked at my shelves of little people and said, "Hmmmm. Interesting that you are making mythical characters." I just smiled, as I didn't know what he was talking about. Weren't these just fun little people? But without my really knowing it, the path made an interesting loop, a quick turn, and my world got bigger. It happened gradually, but I came to understand that I was making little characters that not only made me smile but also told my story. Since each individual story is part of a universal story, so when I tell my story, I tell part of yours as well.

This sounds complicated, but it's really quite simple. There is something about the freedom of creating imaginary beings that invites the child within to come out and play. And playing, it turns out, is the magic portal into creativity. As you make choices about what color of clay to use or what hat or mask to put on a character, you filter it through your own personality, until you create a unique alter ego of sorts, looking back at you in wonder and amusement.

It's quite a trip, so enjoy the journey! I look forward to seeing you along the path.

Maureen Carlson

the Secret Door

the portal into the world of the faerie folk

The Land of the Faerie Folk is everywhere and nowhere at all. Try as you might to get from the ordinary now to the extraordinary there, you cannot. The Secret Door that opens into that magical land simply will not appear. It is not a matter of following a map or buying a train ticket or of saying the right words. To get there is a matter of becoming small.

Not small as in tiny. That won't do, for you are what you are, which is human. And humans are big. But small as in young at heart, small as in innocent and eager to dream new dreams, small as in knowing that you don't have all of the answers to everything that is, or was, or ever will be. It isn't easy to become small, but when you do, the Secret Door swings open. Then you have only to imagine that you are entering through, and it is so.

In fairytales, the words Once Upon a Time are a clue that you are about to escape from the ordinary to the realm of imagination. Think of the fun to be had by combining fairytales with the Secret Door. Make the door, then install it in a special place, using some of the ideas suggested at the end of this project. Then, each time you look at the door, let it become a trigger for your imagination, a portal into the world of fairytales.

materials

Polymer clay: 3 ounces (85 grams) or less of dark brown, light brown, beige, translucent and white

Color recipes:

- For wood clay, roll 2 ounces (57 grams) of light brown clay, 2 ounces (57 grams) of beige clay and 1 ounce (28 grams) of dark brown clay)

- For the door frame, mix together 2 ounces (56 grams) of translucent clay, a $^7/8$" (2cm) ball of beige and of white clay, and a $^1/4$" (6mm) ball of wood clay

Liquid polymer clay

Two hinges, $^5/8$" (16mm) wide and $1^1/8$" (3cm) long

Large (6mm) jump ring

22-gauge copper wire

Aluminum wire mesh, $^1/16$" (1mm) pattern

Piece of fabric or paper towel

Old toothbrush

Paper or parchment

Acrylic paints: brown, green and white

Basic tools (page 12)

Pattern (page 122)

The pictured door and frame is $6^5/8$" (17cm) tall by $5^1/2$" (14cm) wide. Adjust the pattern by enlarging or reducing, then adjusting the measurements and supplies to reflect your changes.

1 Roll the wood clay into 4" (10cm) ropes. Stack the ropes, then roll the stack into a 12" (30cm) rope. Cut the rope into three equal pieces, stack the pieces, then roll to create another 12" (30cm) rope. Repeat until the clay is mixed but you can still see variations in the color. This will create the wood-like texture in the clay.

2 Flatten half of the wood clay into a sheet that is at least 7" (18cm) tall by 5" (13cm) wide and $1/8$" (3mm) thick. Save the rest of the clay for later in the project. Lay the clay on a piece of paper or baking parchment. Trace and cut out the door and door-frame pattern on page 122 from aluminum mesh.

3 Lay the metal mesh pieces on the flattened clay, so the door is inside the frame. Lay hinges in place on the left side of the frame and extended onto the door, adjusting the position of the hinges or door as needed. Use a needle tool to mark where the holes in the hinges are positioned in the clay.

4 Remove the hinges and trim around the door and frame with a craft knife, removing the excess clay. Use a needle tool to create four holes, spaced $1/8$" (3mm) apart, where you would like the handle of the door to be. Check all the holes to make sure they go through the clay and are large enough to accommodate the wires. Bake the door and frame for 20 minutes, following the directions on the package of clay. Let them cool.

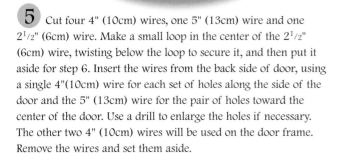

5 Cut four 4" (10cm) wires, one 5" (13cm) wire and one 2¹/₂" (6cm) wire. Make a small loop in the center of the 2¹/₂" (6cm) wire, twisting below the loop to secure it, and then put it aside for step 6. Insert the wires from the back side of door, using a single 4"(10cm) wire for each set of holes along the side of the door and the 5" (13cm) wire for the pair of holes toward the center of the door. Use a drill to enlarge the holes if necessary. The other two 4" (10cm) wires will be used on the door frame. Remove the wires and set them aside.

6 From the front of the door, insert the ends of the looped wire through the two center holes of the door handle and pull until the loop rests against the clay. From the back, bring the ends of the wire back up through the outer holes, pull tight and flatten the ends against the front of the door. Next, flatten the clay you set aside in step 2 into a sheet ¹/₈" (3mm) thick. From this, cut "planks" to cover the door. Brush the door and wire mesh with a thin coat of liquid polymer clay, then press the planks in place, making sure not to cover the wire-loop door handle.

7 Trim the clay edges of the wood planks. Save the excess clay scraps for a future step. Use a knife or needle tool to draw the wood grain. Press gently with a piece of fabric or a paper towel to give texture to the surface. Replace the hinge wires, then bake the door for 20 minutes, following the directions on the package of clay.

8 Fit the door into the frame. Insert the two remaining 4" (10cm) wires through holes in frame. Place the hinges over the wires and onto the baked door and frame. Use pliers to bend and position the wires so that they fit tightly against the back of the door and frame. Trim the wire ends to ¹/₄" (6mm), then use pliers to make loops in the ends of the wire. Make sure the loops are large and tight enough to hold the hinges securely in place.

9 Brush the door frame with liquid polymer clay. Mix the clay for the door frame until marbled. Roll the clay for the door frame into a $3/4$" (1cm) diameter log. To make slices that will fit the curve of the frame, pinch the top of the log so it's slightly triangular. Cut $1/4$" (6mm) slices and fit them around the top of the door and over the frame. Reshape the clay into a squared log, then cut slices to fit along the sides of the frame and the bottom. Add texture by pressing the clay with a stone, toothbrush or crumpled foil. Bake the frame and door for 20 minutes.

10 Roll thin ropes of white clay. Press the ropes between the clay stones, using first a knitting needle and then a brush to smooth the surface. Add white clay around the inside of the door frame as needed to fill gaps. Use an old toothbrush to add texture. Cover the wire loops in the hinges with six $1/8$" (3mm) balls of brown clay. Press them over the loops, then squeeze them in place. Attach a jump ring for the door pull on the wire loop. Make sure the door frame will open, then bake the door and frame for 30 minutes.

11 Mix water and brown acrylic paint in a bowl, then antique the door with a watery coat of the mixture, wiping it away immediately with a dry paper towel. If antiquing is too light, add another wash of paint. If it's too dark, use a wet brush to remove the wash before it dries. For a woodsy, mossy look, use a torn sponge to dab small amounts of green, brown and white paint on the corners and edges of the door.

notes from Woodpecker Pete

If you would like to attach the door to a surface, drill a small hole in each corner so it can be hung or secured on a flat surface.

what lies beyond the secret door

*W*ho should enter your Secret
Door? What's on the other
side? Where does it go? To help
the Faerie Folk, make a little
message to hang beside the door.
Use tiny words if they are for
the Faerie Folk to read, or larger
ones if they are intended for those
human folk who may pass by.

To give a hint as to what lies
beyond the Secret Door, add a real
or artificial vine, some steps made
out of leftover clay and perhaps a
little fairy hat or some shoes.

For information on making
the brown shoes and hat, see the
Annabelle Mae project (page 82).
The striped hat is a variation on
Woodpecker Pete's hat (page 81).

A door with a view

If your Secret Door is to be used indoors, and if there is an opening or mouse hole over which it will fit, you are in luck! If not,
tape or glue a picture to the back of the doorframe. Choose your
favorite outdoor scene. A door with a view is much better than a
blank wall.

Add a sign

To make a sign, flatten wood clay to $1/8$" (3mm) thick. Cut a $7/8$"
x $2^1/2$" (22mm x 6cm) piece for each sign. Lay the clay signs onto
baking paper before you begin. Stamp a message into the unbaked
clay of the sign, using rubber stamps or metal punches. Bake the
sign for 30 minutes. Let it cool. Paint the stamped impression
with watery black acrylic paint, immediately wiping away the
excess with a paper towel. Drill holes in the corners of the sign
for attaching a string.

Ophelia Lilliana

the fairy sprite

So begins the story of Ophelia, one of the smallest of the Faerie Folk.

With a creak, the secret, enchanted door opens into the world of imagination. The sound of a flute and the scent of lavender floats through the air from that world into yours. Next come tiny whispers and tinkling laughter, and then a rustling movement and a glimpse of fluttering wings. In your mind's eye, you turn, just as whatever it is disappears at the edge of the garden.

You aren't sure, but something lingering in the air makes you think of fairies, tiny fairies, the kind that hover at dawn near the periwinkles and drink dew from the tips of the leaves. You look around and recall stories of fairies who gather in chatty groups near the morning glories, swinging their legs over the trellis, waiting for the blossoms to open to greet the day. You breathe in the air, and everything around you feels lighter and full of possibilities.

Celebrate the spirit of these elusive fairies by creating one or more to perch on your desk. Find a special piece of driftwood and perhaps a bit of moss to fashion a seat for them, and prepare to be delighted. You might not be able to capture a real fairy, but you surely can capture the joy and wonder that is their essence.

materials

Polymer clay: 2 ounces (57 grams) or less of translucent, brown, gold, metallic white and flesh color

Color recipes:

- For the clothing, combine 5/8" (16mm) balls of metallic white clay and gold clay

- For hair, combine a 5/8" (16mm) ball of translucent clay with a 1/2" (12mm) ball of brown clay

Instant glue

Fiber fill stuffing, aluminum foil or cardstock

24-gauge tinned copper wire

Beads: four clear glass seed beads; two bugle beads; two 1mm black holeless beads (Note: you may substitute black clay for the black holeless beads.)

Brown acrylic paint

Powdered blush

Basic tools (page 12)

Pattern (page 122)

Ophelia is 3 1/2" (9cm) tall while sitting, and 5" (13cm) if standing.

1 From flesh-colored clay, roll a $^1/_2$" (13mm) ball for the head, roll two $^3/_8$" (9mm) balls for the arms and a $^1/_8$" (3mm) ball for the neck. Roll a $^5/_8$" (16mm) ball for the body and a $^1/_2$" (13mm) ball for each leg from the gold mix clay. Roll the body into a rope that is 1" (25mm) long. Roll your finger over the middle of the body to accentuate the waist. Flatten the shoulders and chest slightly. Shape the shoulders and bust. Press a wire $1^1/_4$" (3cm) long into the body to support the neck.

2 Roll the legs into tapered 3" (8cm) long ropes. For both legs, place your fingers 1" (25mm) from the small end of the leg and make a quick turn for the heel. Use your fingers to roll and shape the ankle. Curve the foot and roll the toes if desired. Stretch the clay slightly to give the ankle a graceful curve. Make a quick turn for the knee. To shape the knee and calf, use your two pointer fingers to hold the leg. Gently roll the area just below the knee, then smooth the knee and calf.

3 Rolls the arms into tapered $1^1/_2$" (4cm) long ropes. Place your fingers $^1/_2$" (13mm) from the small end of each arm and roll the wrist. Flatten the hand slightly. Use a knife to cut out the thumb. Use a small knitting needle to smooth the area around the thumb and fingers. Indent the hand on the palm side at the wrist and across the middle of the hand. Make quick turns at the elbows. (See Creating Sharp Bends on page 17.)

4 Press the arms and legs to the body. Use a toothpick to press two holes into the fairy's back for the wings. Place the fairy onto a square-edged pan or support so that her legs hang down. Prop her legs and arms so that they will hold their position while baking. Be sure the limbs are straight from shoulder to elbow, elbow to wrist, hip to knee and knee to ankle. Bake the body for 20 minutes, following the directions on the package of clay. Let the clay cool.

5 For the neck, press a ⅛" (3mm) ball of clay over the neck wire, adjusting the angle if necessary. Roll the head into an egg shape. Press the pointed end of the egg against your work surface to create a chin. Make a mouth using a blunt needle tool. Indent the corners of the mouth with a small, blunt needle. Smooth the indentations with your fingers or a brush. For the nose, press a tiny oval of flesh-colored clay in place. Blend the edges with a knitting needle and brush. For eyes, press tiny, holeless black beads in place. Use a needle tool to indent the corners of the eyes. Place the head on the neck. If you like, add a little powdered blush to the cheeks.

6 Press tiny flattened teardrops of flesh-colored clay to the sides of the head for ears. Use a rounded tool to indent the center of each ear.

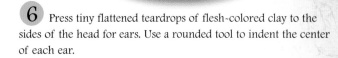

8 Cut two 4½" (11cm) lengths of 24-gauge wire. Make a loop in the center of each wire by wrapping the wire around a toothpick. Lay the wires over the wing pattern on page 122. Shape the wire to create an outline of the wings, then twist the ends of the wire together to close the loop. Trim the ends to ¼" (6mm) long.

7 Roll the clay for the hair into a 3" (8cm) long rope. Flatten the rope to ⅟₁₆" (2mm) thick, then trim to ¾" (19mm) wide. Use a knife to cut the clay into narrow strips. Pick up strips, several at a time, and twist into curls. Press the sections to the head, beginning with the back of the head. To add pieces on top, wrap the end of the hair over a needle, then press it in place. Bake the fairy for 20 minutes, propping it as needed (see page 37 for more information on propping). When cool, paint tiny eyebrows using brown acrylic paint.

notes from Woodpecker Pete

For a surprised expression, use a toothpick to create a round mouth. For an open smile, use a small needle tool to create a hole, then press the tool up in each corner of the mouth. Use a patting motion of your fingers to gently close the corners, then indent the corners with a needle tool.

9 Flatten a sheet of translucent clay to $^1/_{16}$" (2mm) thick. Lay the wire wings on the clay, then cover the wires with a second sheet of $^1/_{16}$" (2mm) thick translucent clay. Use a knife to trim around the wire wings. Press the wings between your palms to flatten the edges, then trim the edges with small scissors. Make sure the loops at the end of the wire are uncovered. Curve the wire slightly. When you are satisfied with the shape of the wings, bake the wings for 20 minutes, following the directions on the package of clay. Let the wings cool.

10 To make bead dangles, cut two 1" (3cm) wires. For each dangle, use flat- or round-nosed pliers to make a loop on one end. Thread beads on the wire in this order: one seed bead, one bugle bead and one seed bead. Make a second loop at the other end of the wire. To attach dangles to wings, open one loop on each dangle just enough to slip the dangle over the wing loop. Then close the loop.

11 Use instant glue to fasten the wing wires to the holes in the body.

notes from Woodpecker Pete

If you are using a brand of clay that scorches easily with repeated baking, you can bake the neck and head separately, then glue them onto the already-baked body using instant glue.

a spriggle of sprites

a single sprite is a lonely sight. Sprites enjoy the company of other creatures of the forest and are rarely found alone. Gather enough sprites together and you have what is known as a spriggle of sprites.

When you create a sculpture, you have to consider not only its shape but also its form, or how it fills up space. It will be viewed not only from the front but also from the sides. Look at each side to see if the angle is pleasing before you put your fairy in the oven. Make sure the clay is supported or you may end up with a sad sprite!

Supporting the arms

Uplifted arms may sag in the oven. To support arms, insert a wire through the shoulders. Cut the wire long enough to go from elbow to elbow, or from elbow to opposite shoulder if only one arm is raised. Insert the wires and bake the body first, then bend the wires to the correct angle and add the arms over the wire. Make sure you support the lower half of the arm during baking.

Supporting the body

When you are ready to bake, prop the fairies to keep their arms and legs in position. Check the fairy from all sides to be sure that the "bones" look straight. You won't be able to make quick adjustments once the clay is baked. If needed, reposition and add extra fiber fill or aluminum foil as a prop. Larger items, such as ceramic coffee mugs, will keep the "bones" of the fairy straight.

Oakheart Will
the spirit of the trees

There is a magic and a mystery about trees. Every gardener who grieves over a fallen limb after a spring storm, and every walker who wanders down forest paths, knows that this is true. Every tree has a story to tell, if we human folk would stay still long enough to listen. Perhaps that is the real reason you often find a bench beneath a tree.

Look at the way the light of late afternoon plays against the bark of the willow to reveal an aged crone hidden beneath the surface. Do you see how the burl in the small twisted oak becomes a wise face with a crooked grin?

How can you doubt the personality and spirit of trees once you see the evidence? You have only to close your eyes and listen to imagine the conversation in the midst of the pines or the songs that drift down from the willow.

Imagine the personality of the oak in your backyard or of an apple tree in your grandmother's orchard. Mix clay to match the color of its bark, then make a face for the tree so that next time you come to visit, you might sit down and have a regular chat!

materials

Polymer Clay: 8 ounces (227 grams) of scrap clay, plus 2 ounces (57 grams) or less of beige, black, dark brown, copper and white

22-gauge copper wire

Aluminum foil

Cardstock or baking parchment

Distressing tools, such as an old toothbrush, crumpled foil, piece of real bark or a stick

Pasta machine

Basic tools (page 12)

The size of each piece in this project is:

Eyebrows: $4^{1}/2''$ (12cm) wide and $^{3}/4''$ (2cm) tall at the center

Eyes: 3'' (8cm) wide and $2^{1}/4''$ (57mm) tall at the center

Nose: $2^{1}/2''$ (63mm) wide at the base and 5'' (13cm) tall

Mouth: 5'' (13cm) wide and $2^{1}/2''$ (63mm) tall at the center

notes from Woodpecker Pete

There's no need to follow these steps exactly. The size may be adjusted by using more or less clay. Large faces should be made over a foil armature to decrease the amount of clay used. Don't hesitate to experiment with different mixes of clay and facial expressions. Every tree is different, so try to match the color of clay with the tree, then find an expression to match the tree's personality.

39

1 Mix 8 ounces (227 grams) of scrap clays to create a uniform brownish color. For the nose, roll a $1^5/_8$" (4cm) ball into a teardrop shape. Create the ridge of the nose by softly pinching along the top side of the teardrop. Press the rounded ball of the nose against your work surface to flatten slightly both the back and bottom. Indent the area just above the nostrils by pinching it. Pat and pull out the ball of the nose, then flatten the nostril area slightly by pressing it with your thumbs. Use a knitting needle to indent the nostrils.

2 For each eyeball, roll a 1" (25mm) ball of beige clay and a $^3/_8$" (9mm) ball of dark brown clay. Press the center of the beige ball with a rounded, $^1/_2$" (13mm) wide clay tool. Drop the brown ball into the center of the beige eye, then press the center of the brown ball with a smaller rounded clay tool. To make eyelids, shape four 1" (25mm) balls of brown clay into footballs, then flatten them into half-moon shapes. Lay one under and one over each eye, overlapping the corners slightly.

3 To make lips, roll two $1^1/_8$" (28mm) wide balls of brown clay into football shapes, then flatten them into half-moon shapes that are thicker in the middle than at the ends. Indent the center of the bottom lip and stretch the ends. Indent the bottom edge of the top lip on either side of the center. Indent the center of the top edge of the top lip. Smooth and round all the edges. Connect the two lips together by overlapping the edges.

4 Lay the eyes, nose and mouth on paper or parchment to check the relationship of the parts, and make adjustments as needed to the size and shape. To make eyebrows, roll two $^7/_8$" (22mm) balls of clay into tapered ropes 4" (10cm) long. Make a bend in the eyebrows at a point $2^1/_2$" (63mm) from the wide end.

6 To make bark-colored clay for this tree, roll the following clay into 3" (8cm) long ropes: a $^7/_8$" (22mm) ball of dark brown, a $1^1/_8$" (28mm) ball of copper, a $1^1/_4$" (31mm) ball of beige, a $^1/_2$" (13mm) ball of white and $^1/_2$" (13mm) ball of black. Lay the ropes together, then twist and mix slightly. Flatten the clay with a roller or pasta machine to a $^1/_8$" (3mm) thickness. Cut the sheet in half, putting aside one half. Fold the remaining clay in half and flatten again. Repeat, keeping the side you like best on the outside with each fold, until you are satisfied with the pattern. Flatten it to a sheet $^1/_{16}$" (2mm) thick. Repeat the process with the other half.

5 Cut nine $2^1/_4$" (6cm) lengths of wire. Bend each wire in half, then twist each into a center loop. Twist the tails together to create a second small loop. Lay the wires on the back sides of all the face pieces, using one for each eye and the nose, and two for each eyebrow and the mouth. Position the wires so that the smooth loops almost reach the top edge of each piece. To hold the wires in place, press a $^3/_8$" (9mm) ball of clay over the bottom loop and the cut wire ends. Cover the top loop with aluminum foil to keep it from embedding in the clay.

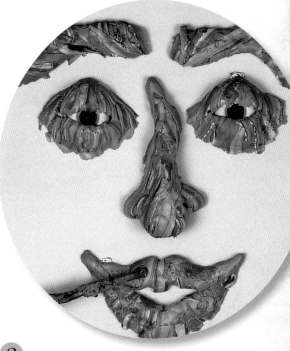

8 Distress the surface of the clay bark by pressing it with an old toothbrush, crumpled foil or a piece of real bark. Use a stick to press knotholes in the surface. Bake the features for 30 minutes, following the directions on the package of clay. Let them cool. Hang the face on a tree using the hooks in the back.

7 Place the face pieces on cardstock or baking parchment. Tear small, thin strips from the bark-colored clay sheet you made in step 6. Cover all the face pieces with layers of patterned clay so it resembles bark.

41

The Green Man

the spirit of green and growing things

The Faerie Folk would still be Faerie Folk if there were no gardens and no forests. But they would certainly not dance the same dances, nor would they sing the same songs. Without green and growing things, they would become slow and silent like twigs that have fallen in a storm—still useful, but without life or vitality. Because they know that their lives depend on green and growing things, they honor the spirit of all that is green by telling the story of the Green Man.

According to their legends, the Green Man sends his energy through everything that grows, including every tree in the forest and every vine that climbs a garden wall. It is rumored that his laughing smile can sometimes be glimpsed within the evergreen or behind the daffodils, but no one knows for sure if it is true. What is known is that there is a life and energy in everything that grows, and, for that, the Faerie Folk give thanks.

Honor the green and growing things in your life by making a Green Man face to hang on your garden wall. Let it remind you that it is wise to protect the earth and all that grows, for, just like the Faerie Folk, our very lives depend on it.

notes from Woodpecker Pete

If you are new at sculpting faces, then the Green Man project is perfect for learning and practicing your sculpting skills. It is much easier to make a large face than it is a small one. Practicing your face skills and completing a project at the same time is both fun and useful. Once you learn the basic steps, practice making a smaller face by reducing the size of each of the parts.

materials

Polymer clay: 6 ounces (170 grams) of scrap clay, 4 ounces (114 grams) of beige, 3 ounces (85 grams) of caramel and green, 1 ounce (28 grams) of gold and a small amount of dark brown and black for eyes

Color recipes:

- For the flesh-colored clay, mix 3 ounces (85 grams) each of beige and caramel clay, or choose your own skin color

- For the leaves, mix 1 ounce (28 grams) of gold clay with 3 ounces (85 grams) of green clay

4¼" x 5¾" (11cm x 15cm) piece of woven or expandable aluminum mesh

9" (23cm) of 22- or 24-gauge copper wire

18" (46cm) of 18-gauge green florist wire

36" (91cm) of 22- to 32-gauge green florist wire

Small twigs and leaves

Aluminum foil

Acrylic paint: white

Sealer (see page 13 for more information)

Paintbrush

Garden gloves

Basic tools (page 12)

The Green Man is 7½" (19cm) long and 6" (15cm) wide. He is a little over 2" (5cm) thick at his nose.

1 Wad a 2' (61cm) sheet of aluminum foil into a loose egg shape. Press the aluminum foil against your work surface to make the back side flat. Press the sides together to create a $3^1/2$" (9cm) wide by 5" (13cm) tall by 1" (3cm) deep face. Use a rounded tool to press in eye sockets just above the center of the face.

2 To make the nose, tear off a 4" (10cm) piece of foil. Wad it into a teardrop, then press it against your work surface to flatten the back and the large end. Press the sides to create a very skinny nose shape. Lay the nose on the foil face, between the eyes. To hold the nose in place, cover the entire face and nose with another sheet of foil, following the contours of the eyes and nose.

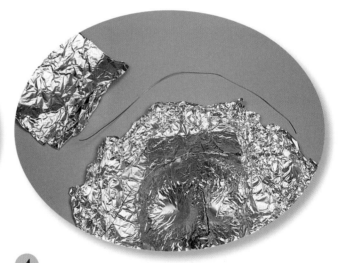

3 It is a good idea to wear garden gloves as you work with mesh. Lay the face on top of the aluminum mesh. Measure approximately $^3/4$" (19mm) beyond the edge of the face. Use old scissors to cut the mesh on the measurement. Use pliers to bend the edge of the mesh back so the edges aren't sharp. Press the edges flat against your work surface. Press the mesh over the foil face, using a rounded tool to force the mesh into the contours of the face. Remove the mesh from the foil face and set aside.

4 Cover the foil face with another, larger piece of foil to keep the clay from sticking to your work surface. Make a wire hanger for the Green Man from a 9" (23cm) copper wire. Fold a piece of foil over the center of the wire to keep it from embedding into the back of the clay face. Lay the foil-covered wire over the forehead of the face.

5 Roll 6 ounces of scrap clay into a sheet that is ¹/₈" (3mm) thick. Lay the sheet over the face. Press the clay to fit and force out any air bubbles. Trim the edge of the clay close to the foil face.

6 Press the mesh mask firmly over the scrap clay covered face, embedding it slightly in the clay surface. Push the ends of the wire you used in step 4 through the back side of the clay, up through the left and right temples and through the mesh. Pull the extra wire through and curl the ends into a loop. Cover the wire ends with scrap clay to hold them in place. Flatten the flesh-colored clay to a ¹/₈" (3mm) thick sheet, then cover the face with the clay, pressing it to fit the contours.

7 Be sure that all air bubbles are either cut open or forced out to the edges of the flesh-colored clay, then trim the edges of the clay, saving the extra for later in the project. Smooth the surface with your fingers or a rolling tool. Use a needle tool to draw the facial features in the clay.

8 Shape pieces of clay for the facial features. The following measurements were used for this face: *Forehead:* one 1¹/₈" (28mm) ball of flesh-colored clay rolled into a rope, then a barbell shape. *Eyelids:* four ⁵/₈" (16m) balls of flesh-colored clay, rolled into footballs; *Cheekbones:* two ⁵/₈" (16mm) balls of flesh-colored clay, rolled into footballs; *Cheeks:* two 1" (25mm) balls of flesh-colored clay, rolled into long teardrops. *Lips:* two ⁷/₈" (22mm) balls of flesh-colored clay, rolled into long footballs, then turned slightly; *Chin:* one 1¹/₁₆" (27mm) ball of flesh-colored clay, rolled into a football, then flattened slightly; *Nostril:* two ¹/₂" (13mm) balls of flesh-colored clay.

Lay each feature on top of the face lines to check the sizes. Add or remove clay as needed.

9 Remove all the facial features, then begin building up the face by adding the forehead, cheekbones and chin. Flatten each piece slightly before adding it to the face, then blend and smooth it into place using your fingers and a rolling tool, such as a large knitting needle.

10 To shape the cheeks, bend the teardrop-shaped cheek pieces into comma shapes, then flatten them. The top inside edge of the cheek should fit against the sides of the nose, just above the nostrils. The long part of the cheek should stretch down beside the chin. To shape the lips, flatten one long edge, leaving the opposite edge fuller and more rounded. The rounded edges will become the actual lip, while the rest will blend toward the nose or down to the chin. Press an indentation above the full part of the top lip.

11 Lay the lips and cheeks in place. Trim off places that overlap, such as at the corners of the lips and below the nose. Add the balls of clay for the nostrils. Blend edges with a rounded tool, then smooth with your fingers.

12 Check the side profile to see if you need to add more clay to the nose, chin or brow. Add clay as needed. Refine the lips by rolling the clay toward the mouth. This will make the lips more rounded. Indent the corners of the mouth by pressing them with a rounded tool.

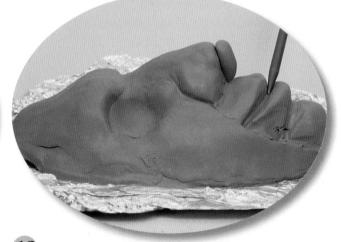

notes from Woodpecker Pete

Don't finish blending any one area of the face before moving on to the next, as each piece that is added will change the rest of the features. Leave the final smoothing until the last step.

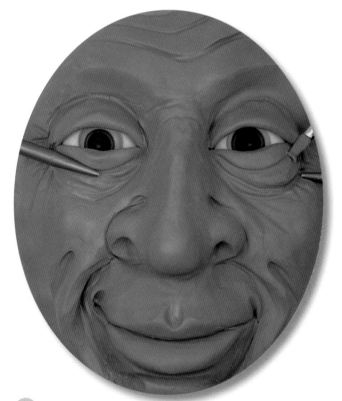

13 Shape the nostrils with a rounded tool. Press in and up to create a rounded nostril. To make the eyes, place one beige $3/4$" (19mm) ball in each eye socket. Press the center of the eyes with a rounded tool to make an indentation. Drop $1/2$" (13mm) dark brown clay ball into the centers of the eyes for the irises. Indent the centers of the irises with a small rounded tool. Drop a $1/8$" (3mm) black ball into the center of each eye for the pupil.

14 Use a needle tool to mark the corners of the eyes. Flatten the football-shaped eyelids to fit from corner to corner of each eye. Lay the lower lids in place, then the upper ones. The lids should curve over and under the eyeballs, not just lay in front of them. Blend the edges of the lids. Refine the shape of the nose and lips by smoothing the clay and cleaning up the lines between the lips with the edge of a thin needle tool.

15 To make the face look friendlier, deepen the smile lines from the corners of the mouth to just above the bottom of the nose. Push the corners of the mouth deeper into the face, as if the lips are stretching around the teeth. Raise the nostrils a bit and make the top of the cheeks fuller; this will add wrinkle lines under the eyes. Add crow's-feet around the corners of the eyes, then smooth the area between the brows and raise the brows slightly. Soften lines with a clay brush.

16 Check the profile. Look from the chin to the forehead and from the forehead to the chin to see if the face looks balanced. To further check for irregularities, view the face upside down or in a mirror. Do a final smoothing with your fingers, a rolling tool and a clay brush. Add texture by pressing a cloth or a paper towel against the face.

17 Once the face is completed, choose twigs and vines to frame the face. Vine tendrils can be made by curling wires around a knitting needle. Flatten the leaf-colored clay to a sheet ⅛" (3mm) thick and cut irregular leaf shapes. Flatten the leaves between your palms, then bevel the edges by rolling your palm over the edge of the leaf. To add texture, press the clay leaf against a real leaf.

18 Press one row of clay leaves along the side of the face. Lay twigs and curled wire vines on top of the leaves. Hold the twigs and vines in place by pressing a small rope of clay over each one.

20 Bake the face for 45 minutes, following the directions on the package of clay. Let it cool, then remove the foil from the back. To bring the character to life, add a dot of white paint to the top right side of each black pupil. Brush gloss lacquer over the center of each eye. This will help ensure the pupil stays in place.

19 Make small clay leaves, following the directions in step 18 and press one over each rope of clay. Use a needle tool to position the leaves in hard-to-reach areas.

the spirits of the seasons

*t*here is a cycle to all of life, including green and growing things. Reflect on these changes by making a sunny face for summer and an earth-toned face for fall. Then make a face without any leaves at all to reflect the promise of winter, that leaves and growing things will truly come again.

It is easy to create variations of the Green Man by using different colors of clay and a variety of face and leaf shapes, or by omitting the leaves completely. Otherwise, each of these faces was made exactly the same as the Green Man in the project.

Autumn
Use copper clay for the face and green and gold for the leaves. Notice that the eyes are also copper.

Summer
Make the face round, and use golden yellow mixed with jasper-colored or pale brown clay for the face. The leaves are various mixes of yellow, brown and green.

Winter
This Green Man is really green! The winter face reminds us that even though all the leaves have fallen, the spirit of green and growing things is preparing to burst forth into spring.

Broogen Bogge
the rock troll

There are creatures in the Faerie World who breathe and move so slowly that they almost never move at all. They are the Rock Trolls. To get a feel for what their life is like, imagine breathing so slowly that it takes days to breathe in a single breath and just as long to breathe it back out again. With days spent just breathing in and others spent breathing out, there isn't a lot that happens in the life of a Rock Troll, but it happens nonetheless.

I wouldn't know that this story were true if it weren't for Broogen Bogge, a Rock Troll who spends most of his days sitting on the riverbank, just below the garden wall. I first noticed him because of his face, which was so peculiar staring out from a rock like that. As days went on I saw that the rock was slowly moving, so I stilled my breath and paid attention and was rewarded with a smile. And now I know. And it is so.

To remind yourself that there are mysteries everywhere and stories yet untold, make a rock troll to sit upon your garden wall. From that perch, he can watch the world as it goes by, and, when you take the time to stop and breathe along with him, he just might share some of what he sees with you.

materials

Polymer clay: Scrap clay to form the base, plus colors that match the colors in your rock

Color recipes:
Since every rock is a different size and color, exact measurements aren't given. Three separate basic mixes were used for this rock:

- 1 part white, 4 parts orange and 1 part green
- 3 parts translucent and 1 part white
- 1 part brown and 2 parts white

Rock

Fiber fill stuffing

Acrylic paints: white, dark brown and green

Sponge

Paintbrush

Pasta machine

Basic tools (page 12)

The size of Broogen will depend on the rock you choose. This rock troll is 5" (13cm) tall and 3" (8cm) wide.

notes from Woodpecker Pete

Using a rock as a base for a sculpture can really help stretch your imagination. Choose a rock, then look at the natural patterns in the rock, just as you would look at the patterns in a cloud. See if you can find a face or a character. Mix clay to resemble the colors in the rock, then add just enough clay to the rock to make the character more visible. This project may surprise you! Sometimes someone unexpected will just appear in the rock.

1 Imagine where a face might be on the rock you've chosen for this project. On the rock, use a pencil to draw a sketch of the troll inside the rock. This will be just an initial guide. To recreate the texture of the rock, create texture stamps by pressing soft clay against different areas of the rock. Bake the stamps for 30 minutes, following the directions on the package of clay.

2 Press scrap clay firmly around the base of the rock to create a stand, then mix rock-colored clay. Mix only a small amount of clay at a time and take careful notes as you adjust colors. Flatten the clay into thin sheets. Repeatedly roll the sheets through a pasta machine, folding the clay after each pass, until the desired color blend is achieved.

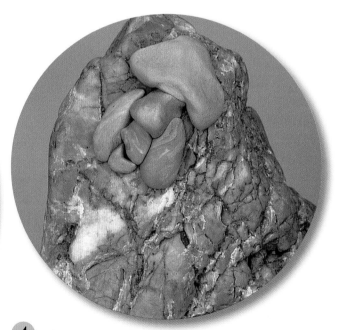

3 Tear off pieces of the blended sheet and press them over the clay stand at the base of the rock. Press the clay stamps you made in step 1 into the rock-colored clay to add texture.

4 From the rock-colored mixes, make shapes for each of the facial features. Press clay over the face or features in the rock. Exact shapes will vary depending on the features in your rock, but ones to consider are: *Forehead:* a rope, flattened into a rectangle, with indentations for brow bones; *Nose:* a teardrop, pressed into a triangular cone; *Cheeks:* a flattened teardrop; *Lips:* a short cone, flattened, with one thicker edge; *Chin:* a flattened short cone; *Ears:* a teardrop, flattened, with an indentation pressed into one side; *Eyelids:* two flattened footballs; *Eyes:* two clay balls.

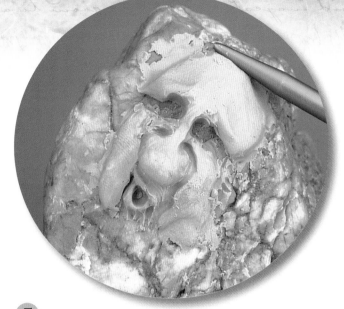

5 Use a knitting needle and your fingers to blend and shape the features. Blend the edges of the clay into the rock. Scrape away the extra clay as you blend it into the rock.

6 Add eyeballs, eyelids and an ear. Press a blunt needle into the eyeballs to create pupils. Add finishing touches to the expression. Smooth the edges with a clay brush and add texture with your stamps.

8 Antique the clay with a watery dark gray, green or brown acrylic paint. Use a dry brush and a sponge to add highlights of color to the rock, blending the edges of the paint. Remove excess paint with a paper towel.

7 Add hands and feet, if you like. Create the hands and feet following the instructions on page 20 and 21, using the rock-colored clay. Because this is a rock, it's okay to leave the hands and feet rough. Blend the edges and add texture as you did for the face. Lay the rock on top of fiber fill stuffing on a baking sheet or tile. Bake for 45 minutes, following the directions on the package of clay. Let it cool.

notes from Woodpecker Pete

Colors that are opposite on the color wheel, such as green and red, will make varying shades of brown when mixed together. If you are mixing by hand, mix each formula separately, then blend them together to make a marbled mix.

Theodore Funguy

the toadstool gnome

The Faerie Folk, being mischievous and slightly mysterious, love to hide. They hide from each other, but also from the human folk who pass their way—so close and yet so unaware. Chances are you've heard their tinkling giggles and thought it was just a sudden chorus of crickets or the buzz of bees.

None are better at this hiding game than Theodore Funguy, the Toadstool Gnome. What makes him so clever is that he hides in plain sight, yet his hiding place is so strikingly beautiful that you'd never expect to find a gnome behind it all. He disguises himself as a stately mushroom. He wriggles into the stem, then pulls on the cap and settles down to wait for a curious passerby. When someone bends down to get a closer view, he looks them in the eye and laughs before he disappears from sight.

Now that you know his trick, you'll have to walk more slowly and look more closely next time you spy a fairy ring. And remember to never again step on a mushroom without first bending over to see what might be hiding there.

Make a Toadstool Gnome to place in a flower pot, a window box or in your garden. Each time you see it, remember that imagination, play, humor and laughter can often be found in the most unexpected places.

notes from Woodpecker Pete

A thin veneer of clay is a good way to save on clay costs. Use leftover or muddied clays to build up the bulk part of a project, then use a thin sheet of new or special colors to cover just the surface.

materials

Polymer clay: 6 ounces (170 grams) of scrap clay, 3 ounces (85 grams) of beige, 2 ounces (57 grams) of yellow, 1 ounce (28 grams) each of white and translucent, and a small amount of green and black for the eyes

Color recipes:
- For the white-mix clay, mix 1 ounce (28 grams) each of white, beige and translucent clay
- For the muted yellow clay, mix $1^1/_2$ ounces (43 grams) each of yellow and beige clay

Liquid polymer clay

6" (15 cm) circle of woven or expandable aluminum mesh

10" (25cm) copper pipe, $^5/_8$" (2cm) diameter

Washer with $^7/_{16}$" (11mm) diameter hole

$2^1/_2$" x $^5/_{16}$" (6cm x 8mm) carriage bolt

$^5/_{16}$" (8mm) nut or two-part epoxy

Aluminum foil

Acrylic paints: coral, white and brown

Matte medium or blending gel (for use with acrylic paints)

Grater for clay

Garden gloves

Paintbrush

Basic tools (pages 12)

Optional: Pastel chalk

The finished Toadstool Gnome is $7^1/_2$" (19cm) tall and $6^1/_2$" (17cm) wide, with $3^1/_2$" (9cm) of exposed pipe at the bottom.

1 Wear garden gloves to protect your hands, as the mesh may be sharp. Cut a 6" (15cm) circle from a sheet of aluminum mesh. Stretch the center of the circle with your thumbs or a large rounded tool to form a cap shape. Make pleats in the sides to keep the shape rounded. For safety, use pliers to bend the edges of the circle up. To smooth the edges, press the mesh against your work surface.

2 Cut a 1/4" (6mm) hole in the center of the mesh cap. Insert a bolt through the hole, then add a washer. Use two-part epoxy to attach the bolt, washer and mesh together, or use a nut to fasten the pieces together. Note: gluing the parts together, rather than using a nut to hold them, will result in a better fitting cap.

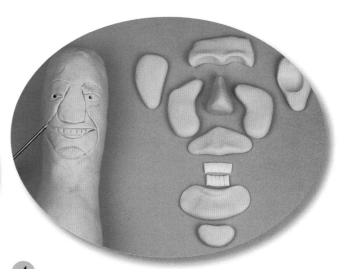

3 Loosely crumple a 1' (30cm) section of aluminum foil. Wrap it around the copper pipe, leaving the bottom 3 1/2" (9cm) of the pipe uncovered. This section will be inserted into the ground. Add more foil as needed to create a wider belly and face armature on the pipe. To smooth the foil, press and roll it against your work surface. Flatten scrap clay into a sheet 1/8" (3mm) thick, then wrap the foil with a single layer of scrap clay. Flatten the white-mix clay to a sheet 1/16" (2mm) thick. Layer the white mix over the scrap clay on the pipe. Blend the seams and smooth the surface.

4 Draw a face on the toadstool with a needle tool. From white-mix clay, roll approximate shapes for each of the facial features: *Forehead:* 3/4" (19mm) ball, flattened into a rectangle with indentations for the brows; *Nose:* 5/8" (16mm) ball, shaped into a teardrop, then pressed into a triangular cone; *Cheeks:* two 5/8" (16mm) balls, flattened into lopsided teardrops; *Lips:* two 5/8" (16mm) balls, flattened into triangles with one thicker edge; *Chin:* 1/2" (13mm) ball, flattened to a half circle; *Ears:* two 5/8" (16mm) balls, flattened to teardrops with an indentation pressed into one side.

From white clay, roll a 1/4" (6mm) flattened rope. Cut two 1/2" x 1/4" (13mm x 6mm) strips, then use a knife to cut teeth lines into the bottom edge of the strips.

5 Lay the parts of the face over the face lines in this order: bottom teeth, top teeth, bottom lip, top lip, nose, chin, forehead, cheeks and ears. Overlap the top teeth over the bottom teeth. Trim all other parts so that the edges touch. Deepen the eye socket with a rounded tool.

6 Use your fingers and a needle tool to blend and sculpt the parts of the face. Smooth and blend the seams.

7 Stretch the ears, broaden the nostrils and indent the chin. Shape the parts of the eye: *Eyes:* two ¹/₄" (6mm) white balls of clay; *Iris:* two ¹/₈" (3mm) green balls of clay; *Pupil:* two ¹/₁₆" (2mm) black balls of clay.

Highlight the pupil with two tiny (as small as you can make them) balls of white clay. Assemble the eyes in the sockets. Roll a ⁵/₁₆" (8mm) ball of white-mixed clay for each eyelid. Flatten them into half circles and stretch the corners. Lay one under and one over each eye. Tuck the ends into the corners of the eyes. To make hair, flatten strips of white-mix clay. Tear the edges and press them in place on the top and sides of the head, being sure to keep the hole in the pipe open.

8 Use a clay brush to smooth and finish the face. Add texture to the toadstool stem by making short, firm strokes with the clay brush. Set the mesh cap on the head, inserting the bolt into the pipe. Make adjustments as needed so the cap fits the head. Remove the mesh cap and bake the pipe and head in a preheated oven for 45 minutes, following the directions on the package of clay. Let the clay cool.

9 Cut a 6" (15cm) circle from a sheet of $^1/_8$" (3mm) thick scrap clay, and a 6" (15cm) circle from a $^1/_{16}$" (2mm) thick sheet of the white-mix clay. Press the circles together, then use them to cover the bottom side of the wire mesh, with the white-mix clay on the outside. Press the clay firmly in place. Curl the edges over the side of the cap. Blend the edges into the mesh, working carefully to avoid sharp wire edges. Use the back of a knife to make gill lines in the clay, then bake the cap in an oven for 30 minutes following the directions on the package of clay. Let the clay cool.

10 Place the cap on the toadstool. Flatten the muted yellow clay to a sheet $^1/_{16}$" (2mm) thick. Cut a 6" (15cm) circle from this clay, and a $5^1/_2$" (14cm) circle from scrap clay. Press the circles together, then lay them on the cap with the muted yellow on top. Press and stretch the edge of the clay so it hangs over the cap slightly. Rip the edges, being sure that the scrap clay doesn't show.

11 Brush liquid polymer clay over the mushroom cap, then grate cold white clay into tiny shreds and add them to the top of the cap. Use a brush to gently press the shreds in place. Remove the cap and bake it for 45 minutes, following the directions on the package of clay. When cool, antique, then mix a tiny bit of coral paint with matte medium or blending gel. Dab color onto the cheeks, nose and chin. Use white paint and a nearly dry brush to highlight areas of the toadstool.

the toadstool court

everyone likes company sometimes, even trolls and toadstools! Make companion toadstools
so that you can display Theodore
with his friends. You could vary
the height, color, width and per-
sonalities of the mushrooms to
create a whole fairy ring. To make
the process easier, create some
without faces. The process for
building the faceless mushrooms is
the same, except the caps may be
smaller or even closed completely.
If the cap fits against the stem, it
doesn't need the mesh for support,
so you can eliminate it and make
the mushroom all in one piece.

Dependable Stan, the Silent Sentinel
Sometimes leftover clay makes the most beautiful marbled hues—perfect for fantasy
mushrooms. This one is shades of beige, brown, rust, granite and gold mixed together.

Gaudy Gabe,
the Toadstool Dandy
Stretch your imagination and create a
colorful fantasy mushroom. This one looks
a bit like a psychedelic pizza. Rolls of layered clay were sliced to create "pepperoni"
pieces that were placed on top of a multi-
colored cap created from scrap clays. The
finishing touches are red clay balls, shreds
of clay and a topping of liquid polymer
clay to hold it all together. At 16" (41cm)
tall and 12" (30cm) across, it does get
noticed amongst the daffodils!

Humboldt the Fourth
a most curious troll

Most every enchanted forest has a stream running through it. If you stop, very still, and listen, you'll hear the rippling sound of the water as it rushes past rocks and over trees that have fallen into its path. Some of these fallen trees reach all the way across the river and form natural bridges. Over these bridges travel the Faerie Folk on their way to gather berries or to harvest cottonwood fluff or, maybe, just to visit with each other in friendly evening gatherings.

Bridges are very inviting, but there is a danger with bridges, one that visitors to the world of the Faerie Folk need to understand. For, you see, trolls and bridges often come together. Trolls are most themselves in those dark and shaded places where sunlight doesn't reach. They like places that are close to the activities of the forest, yet hidden from view. Places like caves. And overgrown river banks. And bridges. Trolls find it easy to hide in places like that, for their oversized noses, long boney arms, knobby toes and tangled hair are perfectly camouflaged amongst the vines, roots and driftwood that collect along riverbanks. So, when you come to a bridge, do go over it, but be ready for trolls, just in case.

Trolls love to collect bright, shiny things. Consider all of the rings, earrings and coins that you have lost over the years. To keep your troll happy, you might create for him a little cloth bag into which he can place, just on loan, of course, a favorite bit of your jewelry. It's one way to build trust between your world and his.

materials

Polymer clay: 8 ounces (227 grams) of the flesh-colored clay of your choice and a small amount of white for the eyes

1³/₄" (4cm) wide piece of cardboard

8" (20cm) of 18-gauge copper or steel wire

6" (15cm) of 14-gauge steel wire

2' x 6" (61cm x 15cm) strip of fabric for the clothing

Yarn or other fibers for the hair

Fabri-Tac glue or a heavy white glue

Fiber fill stuffing

Aluminum foil

Baby powder or cornstarch

Acrylic paints: brown, black, coral and white

Matte medium or blending gel (for use with acrylic paints)

Basic tools (page 12)

Optional: Pasta machine

Humboldt is 5¹/₂" (14cm) tall, sitting, measured from the base of his spine to the top of his head.

notes from Woodpecker Pete

Making a troll is the perfect way to learn and practice new sculpting skills. Trolls don't have to be beautiful, so pretty much anything that you make will work for a troll. And then there is the dirt. Polymer clay, especially the light colors, seems to act as a magnet for dust, fibers and just plain dirt. All of those things sound like things that a troll would love! As you practice, it does get easier to control both the clay and the dirt. So make a few trolls before moving on to the trickier projects in this book.

1 Measure and mark 1¹/₂" (4cm) from each end of the 6" (15cm) steel wire. At the marks, bend the ends of the wire at a right angle, then into a small loop. Wad a 12" (30cm) sheet of aluminum foil into a loose egg shape. Insert the wire into the small end of the egg so that 1¹/₂" (4cm) of wire extends beyond the foil. Squeeze the foil firmly to hold the wire in place. This will be the armature for the body of the troll. Add foil as needed to accentuate the narrow shoulders and large belly of the troll. Roll the armature on your work surface to smooth the foil.

2 Roll the conditoned flesh-colored clay through a pasta machine on the thickest setting, or flatten it with a rolling tool to a sheet ¹/₈" (3mm) thick. Cover the foil armature with a layer of clay. Blend the seams with your fingers. Roll the body between your hands to smooth the surface. Cover the wire neck with clay. Roll a ³/₄" (19mm) clay ball. Place the ball over the wire loop above the body. Smooth the seams. This ball of clay will support the head, so be sure it is securely attached to the neck.

3 Make an indentation for the belly button, then drop a small ball of clay in the indentation. Add and blend clay as needed to build up the shoulders and bottom of the troll. Add any tattoos or body scars to your troll. Use a long needle to create a hole through the shoulders and hips, going completely through the body. To keep the bottom of the troll from flattening as it bakes, place the body on a mound of fiber fill stuffing on a tile or baking sheet, then bake the body for 30 minutes, following the directions on the package of clay. Let the clay cool.

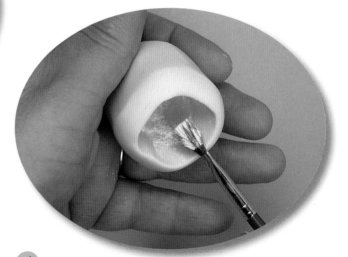

4 Roll a 1³/₄ " (4cm) ball of flesh-colored clay for the head. Use a blunt brush handle or dowel to hollow out the head. Brush a small amount of powder or cornstarch inside the head. This will keep the unbaked clay from sticking to the baked clay neck.

5 Place the head onto the body, pressing it over the baked clay ball of the neck. Squeeze equally all the way around the bottom of the head so the clay armature is "trapped" inside the head. As you continue to sculpt the head, make sure the ball of the neck is still trapped inside the head and that the head still moves. Shape the head to resemble a lopsided egg, with the point of the egg at the chin.

6 Use a needle tool to divide the side of the head in half vertically. Draw the ears behind the line. Draw the face on the front of the head.

7 Check the placement of the features on the face. At this point it's fine, even fun, to make the troll's face lopsided or irregular.

8 Use a rounded tool to press an indentation on each side of the nose to make eye sockets. Roll shapes for the parts of the face: *Brows:* two ¹/₂" (13mm) balls of clay, shaped into half moons; *Nose:* one ³/₄" (19mm) ball of clay shaped into a teardrop; *Cheeks:* two ³/₄" (19mm) balls of clay, flattened into lopsided teardrops; *Lips:* two ⁵/₈" (16mm) balls of clay, flattened into triangles with one thicker edge; *Chin:* one ¹/₂" (13mm) ball of clay, flattened into a half circle.

Position the clay shapes over the corresponding lines on the face, beginning with the nose.

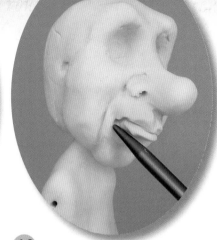

9 Check the profile. Make sure the lips stick out far enough. This will give Humboldt a thoughtful, yet pouty, expression. Note the receding chin as well.

10 Blend and shape the seams by rolling them with a knitting needle and patting and smudging them smooth with your fingers. Indent the nostrils and the corners of the mouth. Note that the bottom edge of the nostrils curl into the nostril holes.

11 Check the general shape of the face, viewing it from all angles. Blend the extra clay toward the back of the head. Trim away or add clay, as needed, to reshape the features.

12 Create the eyes, using two 1/4" (6mm) white clay balls, one for each eye, and four 1/4" (6mm) balls of flesh-colored clay for the eyelids. Drop the white eyeballs into the eye sockets and mark the corners of the eyes. Roll, then press each eyelid into a flattened football shape. Lay the eyelids in place above and below the eyes, beginning with the lower lids. Be sure that the upper lid fits over the top of the eyeball. Blend the edges of the lids slightly, then press in wrinkle lines on the sides of the eyes.

13 Begin each ear with a 3/4" (19mm) ball of flesh-colored clay. Shape the ball into a teardrop, then flatten and roll a rounded tool in the center of the teardrop to shape the ear. Press the ears on either side of the head. Press the ear in place with the blunt end of a rounded tool.

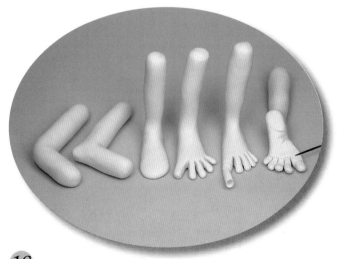

14 For each arm, roll a 1" (25mm) ball of clay into a 3" (8cm) rope. Roll the middle of the rope between your fingers to create a wrist and a 1¹/₂" (4cm) long hand. Flatten the hand into a lopsided paddle, with the hand thicker at the wrist and thinner at the fingers. Cut out an area between the thumb and fingers. Gently pat, press and roll the cut edges and the thumb to create a smooth mitten. Cut three lines in the mitten to create four fingers. Trim the ends, then pat, press and roll the fingers to create a smooth glove shape. Remember to create both a right and left hand.

15 Roll a large needle tool across the center of the palm, then mark creases in the hand, fingers and thumb. Bend the thumb and the area below the thumb toward the center of the hand. Use a piece of drinking straw to make fingernails (see sculpting hands, page 20). Bend the fingers slightly at the knuckles. Note that the bend line for the knuckles is slightly into the back of the hand. Use a knitting needle to press in tendon lines on the back of the hand. Smooth with a clay brush, and bend the fingers at the middle joint.

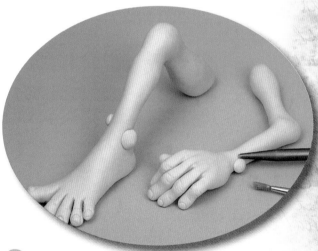

16 Begin each leg with a 1¹/₄" (31mm) ball of flesh-colored clay rolled into a 4" (10cm) rope. Make a soft bend to create a 1¹/₂" (4cm) foot, then make a quick turn to create a bony heel. Stretch the ankle slightly, then flatten the foot so it slopes down toward the toes and the side of the foot, with the big toe longer. Cut four lines in the foot to make toes. Round the toes and make toenails with a straw. On the bottom of the foot, indent an arch on the big toe side of the foot. Add wrinkle lines. Remember to make a right and left foot.

17 Start each arm by rolling and stretching the clay slightly, then bend the middle of the arm to create an elbow. Shape the arm by smoothing it between your fingers. The finished arm, excluding the fingers, is about 3¹/₄" (8cm) long. Repeat with the legs. The finished leg is about 3¹/₂" (9cm) long. To create bones in the wrists and ankles, blend in small balls of clay, one on each wrist and one on each side of the ankles. Exaggerate the knobbiness, if you like. This is a troll!

18 Prop the troll's arms and legs in place, then make a final decision about the position of the knees and elbows. Press a hole through the top of each arm and leg, from side to side. Test the head to be sure that it still turns and that the neck opening is smaller than the size of the ball in the neck. Position the pieces on fiber fill stuffing, then bake in a preheated oven for 40 minutes, following the directions on the package of clay. Let cool.

19 Antique the troll using a wash of brown acrylic paint thinned with water. Wipe the paint off immediately with a paper towel and remove excess paint from the crevices with a wet brush. Repeat as needed. Add age spots by dotting the skin with brown paint and immediately patting dots with a wet finger. Paint the eyes, beginning with a brown iris, a black pupil and finally a white highlight. Let the paint dry between colors. Line the eyes with brown. Paint the eyebrows brown using a nearly dry brush and lifting strokes.

20 Cut the 18-gauge wire into two pieces, one 3 1/2" (9cm) long for the arms and one 4 1/2" (12cm) long for the legs. Use pliers to curl a double loop into one end of each wire. Bend loops at a right angle to the wire. Thread a limb on the wire, then thread the wire through the hole you made in the body earlier, then thread the second limb on the wire. Trim the wire to 1/2" (13mm) beyond the body and use pliers to curl a double loop in the other end of the wire to hold the limbs to the body. Do this for both the arms and legs. Be careful not to put too much pressure on the fragile pieces of clay.

21 To make hair, cut a 1 3/4" (4cm) wide piece of cardboard. Wrap yarn or string around the cardboard 25 to 50 times. Slip the loops from the cardboard, keeping the center circle open. Slip a 3" (8cm) piece of string through the center of the loops, tying them together. Cut the opposite end of the loop from the string, then fluff the hair into a circle so that the tie is at the center. Glue the tie to the top of the head. To dress the troll, wrap a long strip of fabric around the body. Tuck the end under itself to hold the wrap in place.

Heliotrope, a troll of extraordinary beauty

*j*ust because Heliotrope is a troll doesn't mean that she's oblivious to beauty and fashion! In fact, she loves manicures, evidenced by her glamorous blue nails, which, incidentally, match her outfit. Notice that she has earrings to match as well. The earrings were made from tiny balls of blue clay that were baked on a headpin, and then bent to fit her ear. Heliotrope is a troll with true class.

Manicured fingernails

Begin each nail with a teardrop shape. Flatten the teardrop slightly, then press it over a rounded tool to curve the nail. Bake the nails for 30 minutes, following the directions on the package of clay. Make the hands just as you did for Humboldt. Press the baked nails into the tips of the fingers. Remove the nails and brush the tip of the finger with matte liquid polymer clay. Replace the nails and brush with liquid polymer clay. Bake the hands. When cool, brush the nails with gloss lacquer.

Heliotrope's shape

Breasts are added to the body before the body is baked. Start with two 3/4" (2cm) or larger balls of flesh-colored clay. Roll each into a teardrop shape, then slightly flatten the small end. Press the flattened part against the shoulders, then blend it into the chest and shoulders. Finish the rest of the steps the same as for Humboldt, except add longer hair.

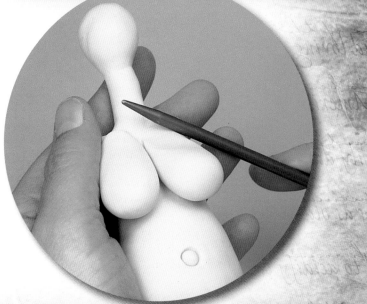

the Forever Tree

The tree spirits Depley Everwhen and Semore Evernow

On the banks of a brook, deep within the heart of Faerie Folk land, there grows a wise old tree known as the Forever Tree. Legend says that it will continue to grow as long as there is one soul in the world who can hear its voice, or voices (to be exact). For this is a magical twin tree, a pair of trees that grew so close together that the trunks merged and became one.

Between the trees, where their bodies have merged, are holes and crevices where visitors may tuck their wishes, questions and dreams. Attending to these requests, on one side of this tree, is Depley Everwhen, a tree spirit who knows all about the dreaming of dreams and the making of plans. On the other side of the tree is Semore Evernow, who gives advice on how to live fully in the here and now. Together, these tree spirits work their magic on visitors so that both the future and the present can be fully lived.

Make a small Forever Tree, then set it on your bookshelf among your favorite books. From time to time, tuck a wish or a dream into a hole or a crevice. You could even build a secret compartment into the tree for receiving those really special dreams.

notes from Woodpecker Pete

The size of your tree may be adjusted by using more or less wire and foil for the armature. Be sure to measure the height, width and depth of your oven and keep the tree within those dimensions.

materials

Polymer clay: 13 ounces (369 grams) of scrap clay, 6 ounces (170 grams) of beige, 6 ounces (170 grams) of dark brown and 2 ounces (57 grams) of white

Color recipe:
• For the bark, mix together 6 ounces (170 grams) each of beige and dark brown clay plus 2 ounces (57 grams) of white clay until finely marbled

8' (2.4m) of 14-gauge wire (coat hanger wire will also work)

1¹/₂' (46cm) of 28-gauge copper wire

Aluminum foil

Acrylic paints: dark brown, white and black

Pasta machine

Old toothbrush

Paintbrush

Basic tools (page 12)

This Forever Tree is 9" (23cm) tall, 11" (28cm) wide and 10¹/₂" (27cm) deep.

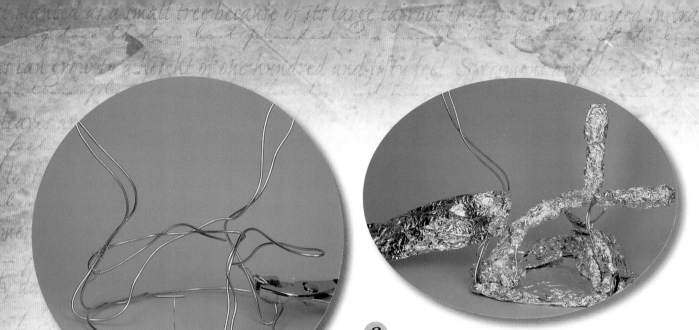

1 Bend one end of the 14-gauge wire into an irregular circle for the base of the tree. Bend the wire up to form three branches for the tree. Use 4" (10cm) pieces of 28-gauge wire to tie together and stabilize the armature at places where two or more wires overlap. If you are using coat hanger wire, be sure to use enough 28-gauge wire to tie together the pieces for support.

2 Tear off a 26" (66cm) piece of foil. Fold it in half, then place it under the wire tree. Fold up the edges to create a base for the tree. Wrap the limbs with additional pieces of foil. Decide where the tree crevices and holes will be. Continue wrapping and filling the limbs and trunk with aluminum foil, leaving spaces for the crevices and holes. The foil tree should be just a little smaller than you want the finished clay tree to be.

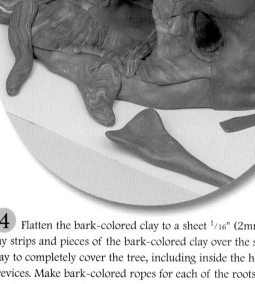

3 Flatten the scrap clay to a sheet 1/8" (3mm) thick sheet using the widest setting on a pasta machine. Cover the base and limbs with the sheet of clay so that no foil is showing. Add more clay as needed to give shape to the tree. Add short clay ropes for the beginning of each root.

4 Flatten the bark-colored clay to a sheet 1/16" (2mm) thick. Lay strips and pieces of the bark-colored clay over the scrap clay to completely cover the tree, including inside the holes and crevices. Make bark-colored ropes for each of the roots. Flatten the first part of each rope, then use the flattened part to cover the scrap clay roots. Stretch and shape each root into twists and curves. Trim the clay base, and use a large knitting needle to blend the seams.

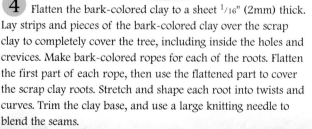

5 Press firmly with an old toothbrush to blend the remaining seams and add texture to the bark. Use a needle tool to add bark lines. You can also press the clay with a piece of real bark or a stamp made from bark.

6 Use a needle tool to draw a face on the tree. Add extra clay as needed to create ridges around the face, then shape each feature using bark-colored clay (except for the eyes): *Forehead:* a ³/₄" (19mm) ball of clay, flattened into a rectangle with indentations on one side for eyes; *Chin:* a ¹/₂" (13mm) ball of clay, shaped into a flattened triangle; *Nose:* a ⁵/₈" (16mm) ball of clay, shaped into a teardrop, then a triangular cone; *Cheeks:* two ³/₄" (19mm) balls of clay, shaped into flattened teardrops, with indentations for eyes; *Lips:* two ³/₈" (9mm) balls of clay, shaped into flattened triangles with one thicker edge; *Eyes:* two ¹/₄" (6mm) balls of white clay; *Eyelids:* two ¹/₈" (3mm) balls of clay shaped into skinny footballs, then flattened; *Foot:* a ¹/₂" (13mm) thick and 4" (10cm) long rope, shaped into a 2" (5cm) long foot at the end of a 2" (5cm) long leg; *Hand:* a ¹/₃" (8mm) thick by 4" (10cm) long rope, shaped into a 1³/₄" (4cm) long hand and a 2¹/₄" (6cm) long arm.

7 Place the clay face pieces over the drawing on the tree. Trim so that the pieces don't overlap. Use a knitting needle and your fingers to blend the features into the tree. Use a brush to smooth and add texture as needed.

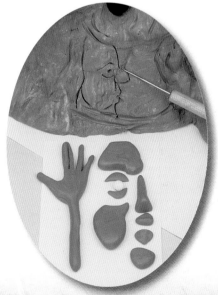

8 Draw a profile face on another side of the tree for a second face. Make shapes just as you did for the first face, except create only half of a face. A leg or hand may be added.

71

9 Lay the face features over the new drawing of a face. Use a knife to trim away the excess clay. Press the point of the nose toward the front edge of the profile.

10 Blend and shape the features, keeping in mind that this is a side view of the face. The features will blend back toward the ear. Do final texturing and shaping of the tree and both faces. Bake the tree in an oven for 45 minutes, following the directions on the package of clay. Let the clay cool.

11 Antique the tree using dark brown acrylic paint that has been watered down. Wipe the paint away immediately, using a paper towel. Wipe away excess paint in the crevices using a dampened brush.

12 If needed, add highlights using light brown or beige paint with a nearly dry brush and a tiny amount of paint. Dab the highlights with a wet paper towel to mute them. Paint the eyes of both faces, using brown acrylic paint for the iris first, then a black dot for the pupil and a white dot for the eye highlight. Let the paint dry between coats.

a home for the fairy

*t*urn the Forever Tree into a more inviting place by adding a door, vines and places for the Faerie Folk to perch. A door and vines will be easier to create and add if the clay tree is baked after the vines are applied and the door is fit to the opening.

The Forever Tree is a perfect perch for other clay characters featured in this book. To make sure the characters will fit on the tree, make the characters first, then shape the tree to fit the characters. Once the tree is shaped, remove the characters and bake the tree.

For more information on making the Sprites found in the tree, turn to page 37.

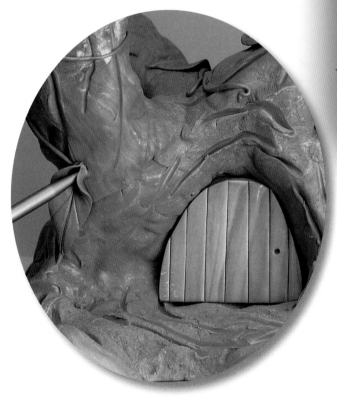

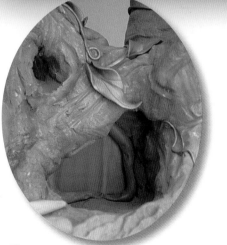

Adding a door and vines

1 Create a door for the tree using brown clay mixed with white and a little gold. Flatten the clay to a sheet 1/4" (6mm) thick. Cut a door shape to fit the cavity in the tree, and cut lines in the door to resemble boards. Bake the door for 30 minutes, following the directions on the package of clay. To make vines, roll thin ropes of green clay and drape them over the tree before the tree is baked. Press them lightly in place. Create leaf shapes from flattened balls of clay, then press them onto real leaves for texture. Press the leaves to the tree, then brush liquid polymer over the leaves to adhere them to the tree, then bake the tree.

2 Fit the baked door in the tree, pressing it into place. From the back of the door, lay a rope of clay to fill any space between the door and the sides of the hole. Smooth the rope into the sides of the tree. This clay will also act as molding around the door opening. Be sure that the door will still open outward. The clay molding will also keep the door from pushing in and getting stuck. Bake the tree again.

Olaf the Wise
a gnome of uncommon wisdom

Olaf the Wise grew up in a family of close-to-the-earth gnomes. Honesty, hard work and loyalty were the standards by which he lived his life. At the end of the day, if the work was stacked neatly in a pile and the floors were swept clean, then he had earned his supper and a night of quiet rest. He didn't expect much more. Life was a bit dull, and there were never any of what you might call adventures, but he had enough to eat and a roof over his head, so all was well.

One day he took a walk through the forest and ended up sitting on a hill to rest. He awoke to find the valley in front of him full of fairies and sprites who flew in great circles and loops. The sheer beauty and joy of the experience made him feel more alive than he ever had before. And he knew that it was good.

When he returned to his village, he still believed in honesty, hard work and loyalty, but he also understood that he needed beauty and play to be whole.

Create your own version of Olaf the Wise to place on your desk where he can listen to your joys and hear your tales of woe. Chances are that Olaf will have some things to say to you as well. An inner voice often needs someone else to make it real.

materials

Polymer clay: 2 ounces (57 grams) or less of flesh color, dark brown, medium brown, ochre, dark blue, white, gold, caramel and dark red

Color recipes:
- For the shirt, mix together 1" (3cm) balls of ochre and white clay
- For the eyes, use two prebaked, 1/4" (6mm) white clay balls

Two 12" (30cm) soft, medium brass rods

Four 5" (13cm) pieces of 28-gauge copper wire

Aluminum foil

Acrylic paints: coral, blue, brown, black and white

Matte medium or blending gel (for use with acrylic paints)

Paintbrush

Basic tools (page 12)

Patterns (page 122)

Optional: Clay softener or liquid polymer clay

Olaf is 7" (18cm) tall from the bottom of his feet to the tip of his hat.

notes from Woodpecker Pete

Medium brown clay will work for the pants, but if you want the pants to have a mottled appearance you can mix a spice such as oregano into light brown clay. Look for pre-mixed clays, such as Jasper Fimo Soft, which also has a mottled appearance, in your local craft stores.

1 Cut ½" (13cm) from both brass rods. Fold one wire in half and lay the folded wire over Trunk Pattern A. Twist the center of the wire to form a 1" (3cm) loop. Use flat-nosed pliers to bend the wire to match the pattern. Lay the second wire over the Trunk and Legs Pattern B, and bend the wire to match the pattern. Use the 28-gauge wires to wrap around the shoulders and hips to secure the two parts of the body together. Twist the ends of the wire.

2 Bend the feet toward the front of the gnome. Adjust the wires so the gnome stands up. Bend the neck forward slightly, then tilt the head up. Tear off a 3" (8cm) strip of aluminum foil. Wad the foil into a loose ball and press it into the center of the body. Use more foil to secure the body armature. Make a small foil egg to fit inside the head armature. Wrap foil around the egg to hold it in place and shape the head. The head armature should be ¼" (6mm) smaller in diameter than the finished head.

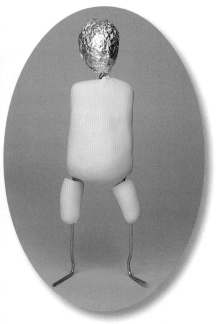

3 Flatten the flesh-colored clay to a sheet ⅛" (3mm) thick. Cover the body with a layer of clay. Add clay as needed to give Olaf a slightly protruding belly, a rounded bottom and a slightly swayed back. Smooth the clay surface. To make thighs, roll two ½" (13mm) thick and ¾" (19mm) long flesh-colored clay pieces. Slice lengthwise halfway through the clay, then press it over the thigh wires. Blend the seam, then bake the armature in an oven for 20 minutes, following the directions on the package of clay. Let it cool.

4 For the head, flatten two 1" (3cm) balls of flesh-colored clay to a sheet ¼" (6mm) thick. Cover the foil head, adding clay or trimming as needed to make an egg-shaped head that is slightly flat in the front. Smooth the clay, then use a needle tool to draw facial features. Use a rounded tool to press in eye sockets. Open the mouth by pressing a needle tool into the clay, then rocking it toward each corner.

5 From a flattened piece of white clay, cut two ¹/₂" x ³/₁₆" (13mm x 5mm) strips of clay for making teeth. Lay strips of clay over a foil-covered round tool, such as a ³/₈" (9mm) dowel. Use a knife to cut in teeth lines, then bake the teeth on the dowel for 20 minutes. Trim as needed to fit the mouth. Make a tongue by mixing a tiny piece of red clay into a ¹/₈" (3mm) ball of flesh-colored clay. Form the clay into a teardrop, then flatten and press it into the mouth, small end first, using a needle tool. Press the baked teeth over the upper lip area. The top of the teeth will eventually be covered with the lip.

6 Use flesh-colored clay to shape the parts of the face: *Forehead*: one ⁵/₈" (16mm) ball of clay, flattened to a rectangle with indentations for the brow bones; *Nose*: one ⁷/₁₆" (11mm) ball of clay, shaped into a teardrop and then pressed into a triangular cone; *Cheeks*: two ¹/₂" (13mm) balls of clay, flattened into lopsided teardrops; *Lips*: two ³/₈" (9mm) balls of clay, shaped into flattened triangles with one thicker edge; *Chin*: one ³/₈" (9mm) ball of clay, shaped into a flattened half circle; *Ears*: two ³/₈" (9mm) balls of clay, shaped into flattened teardrops, with indentations pressed into one side.

Lay the shapes over the face, starting with the bottom lip, then the top lip, nose, chin, cheeks, forehead and ears. Trim the shapes so that the edges touch and don't overlap. Press a rounded tool into the eye sockets to deepen them.

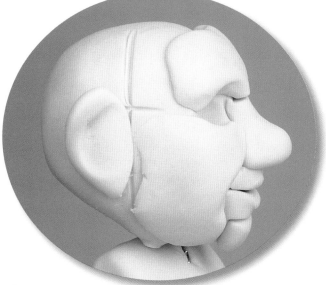

notes from Woodpecker Pete

You can work with unbaked teeth, but baking the teeth first gives you more sculpting freedom, as you don't have to worry about wrecking the shape of the teeth as you sculpt the face.

7 Check the profile. Add or remove clay as needed for the shape of the face.

8 Press prebaked ¹/₄" (6mm) white clay eyeballs into the sockets. Add tiny flattened, flesh-colored footballs for eyelids. Shape the face and bevel the seams by rolling a needle tool toward each seam, then rolling it toward the seam from the opposite side. Smooth the seams, then press a needle into the corners of the mouth and into the nostrils to give more expression. Press the ears to the head with a rounded tool. Shape the eyelids and brow. Add wrinkles and refine the face with a small, sharp needle. Use a clay brush to smooth. If you have difficulty smoothing the face, dip the brush into clay softener or liquid polymer clay. This will make the face sticky until the clay is baked, so do this as a last step.

9 Be sure that Olaf stands on his own. If he doesn't, bend the wires as needed to create balance. Press a ¹/₄" (6mm) wide medium brown clay rope between the legs and up to the waist. Flatten medium brown clay to a sheet ¹/₈" (3mm) thick. Cut out two pants from the clay sheet using the pants pattern on page 122. Each pattern piece makes a leg of the pants. Position the pants on the leg by pressing the center of the pants against the crotch and over the brown clay rope.

10 Bring the edges of the pants around to the sides of the legs. Overlap the front edge over the back edge of the sideseam, then seal the seam carefully. Press the excess clay at the waist into pleats or gathers. Pinch the bottom edge around the knee wire. Repeat with the other leg.

11 For boots, roll two 1" (3cm) balls of dark brown clay into two 2" (5cm) long ropes. Bend softly at the middle, then make a quick turn at the heel. Flatten the toes slightly. Press your finger against the inside edge to create an instep. Hollow out the center of each boot.

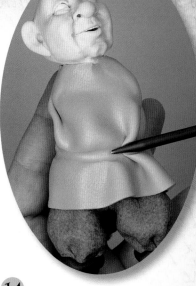

12 Slit the back of the boot, then press the boots over the feet wires. Overlap the boot seams in the back, then blend the seam. Add texture with a piece of fabric to resemble wrinkled leather. If the seam is hard to smooth, wait until you bake the figure, and, when cool, blend more clay into the seam. Feather the edges with a knitting needle, and bake again.

13 Decide on the final position of the head and neck. Add a rope of flesh-colored clay around the wire neck, then blend it into the head and shoulders. Flatten the shirt-colored clay to a sheet $1/8$" (3mm) thick. Cut out a $2^{1}/_{4}$" x 6" (6cm x 15cm) rectangle. Trim the sides so that the top edge is 4" (10cm) wide. Bevel the bottom edge by pressing it between your palms. Add texture with a paper towel or cloth. Wrap it around the figure, overlapping the short sides and sealing the seam.

14 Fit the shirt to the neck by adding pleats. Use a needle tool to create a waist in the shirt.

15 Make a pouch by hollowing out a $5/8$" (16mm) ball of caramel clay. Create a flap by rolling a $3/8$" (9mm) ball of caramel clay into a short rope. Flatten the rope, then press it to the waist with the long side up. Position the pouch over the flap. Make a belt from a flattened $3/16$" (5mm) wide rope of caramel clay. Make a buckle and prong from gold clay rolled into a very thin rope. Press holes in the belt. Add a loop, pressing the end of the loop to the back side of the belt. Place the belt around the waist, pressing the flap down over the belt and pouch. Make a button-hole and add a button.

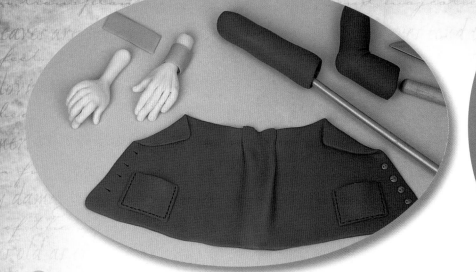

16 For the jacket, flatten blue clay to a sheet $^1/_8$" (3mm) thick. Cut out a $2^1/_2$" x 6" (63mm x 15cm) rectangle, then trim it at an angle so the top edge is 4" (10cm) wide. Cut out and press the pockets in place, then add buttonholes and gold clay buttons. Fold over the top corners of the jacket to create lapels, then add a pleat in the center of the back. Add stitch marks around the pockets with a sharp needle. To create hands, begin with a $^3/_8$" (9mm) ball of flesh-colored clay rolled into a $1^3/_4$" (4cm) rope for each hand, then follow the directions on page 20. Each hand should be 1" (3cm) long. Wrap each wrist with a flat strip of shirt-colored clay. Create two sleeves with ropes that are $2^1/_4$" (56mm) long. Make a quick turn in the middle and taper one end of each sleeve. Hollow out each tapered end to the elbow. Press the hands in place, trimming the arms as needed.

17 Fit the jacket onto Olaf, stretching it as needed to fit. Press on the sleeves, adding both at the same time so that you are pressing from opposite sides. Smooth the tops of the sleeves so they are rounded. Adjust the jacket as needed with a clay brush. Prop Olaf on a baking tray, then bake for 20 minutes, following the directions on the package of clay. Let him cool.

18 On the face, dab blush made from a bit of coral paint mixed with matte medium or blending gel. Paint the eyes. The eyebrows are painted with light, lifting strokes using a nearly dry brush and brown paint. Press strips of white clay (mixed with just a bit of light brown or gold clay if desired) to the head to create the beard, mustache and hair. Use the point of a knife to add lines in the hair. Lift the clay at irregular intervals to break up the downward lines.

notes from Woodpecker Pete

If the mustache feels loose, brush a small amount of matte liquid polymer clay under the mustache and around the edges of the beard.

19 Make a hat from a $1^1/_2$" (4cm) ball of red clay. Roll the ball into a cone shape, then hollow out the cone with a brush handle. Turn the edges under slightly, then fit the hat on the head. Bake Olaf in an oven, propping him once again on a baking tray, for 30 to 40 minutes, following the directions on the package of clay.

Woodpecker Pete

*W*oodpecker Pete, pictured here, is an elf, while Olaf the Wise is a gnome. Despite this difference, it's not hard to make Woodpecker Pete using the directions for Olaf. Some surface differences are easy to notice; the beard and mustache were eliminated for the elf, and the collar was added to Pete's jacket. The color of Pete's clothing was also changed. Various spices were added to create color and the spotty, pebbly effects. The toes of his boots were also stretched into curls, similar to those of Ophelia Lilliana (page 32).

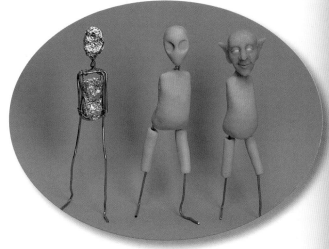

The differences inside

Looking one step deeper, at Woodpecker Pete's armature, you can see more of what makes him different from Olaf. Woodpecker Pete is the same height as Olaf, but his face is smaller and thinner in relationship to his body. It is almost pointed rather than rounded. His body is narrower, his legs are longer and his body is shorter in relationship to his total height.

The differences on top

With a quick stretch, twist and bend, Olaf's pointed gnome hat turns into a hat fit for an elf.

AnnaBelle Mae
the faerie folk storyteller

Ahhh ... now is the time for the storyteller to tell her own story. One might think this tale would be the easiest of all, but stories such as mine are never easy.

Tucked under the gnarled roots of an ancient oak tree is a tiny, moss-covered cottage. Over the door hangs a sign that says *The Storyteller*. If you were to peek through one of the curtained windows, you might even see the storyteller, whose name is AnnaBelle Mae, sitting at her kitchen table. It is not certain if she is an elf, a gnome or a sweet-faced troll.

What is certain is that she is a teller of tales, a weaver of words and a keeper of memories. This you can tell by the concentration with which she writes in the thick journal that is propped open in front of her, and by the piles of scrapbooks, notebooks and papers that fill every nook of the room. Rumor has it that she also tempts human folk into telling their own stories as they enter the world of the Faerie Folk. Perhaps it will happen to you.

Perch the storyteller on a bookshelf next to a pile of your favorite books, along with a journal or a notebook and some pens and pencils. Let her be a reminder that the whole world of the Faerie Folk is as close as your own imagination. You never know when the doorway to the world of Faerie might open. Be ready.

materials

Polymer clay: 2 ounces (57 grams) or less of flesh color, brown, gold, red, translucent, champagne and white

Color recipes:
- For beige-mix clay, mix together 1" (25mm) balls of champagne, translucent and white clay
- For the skirt, mix a 1¼" (31mm) ball of beige-mix clay with a tiny pinch of turmeric and nutmeg
- For the eyes, use two ⅛" (3mm) prebaked white clay balls

Liquid polymer clay

Spices: Paprika, nutmeg, sage, turmeric, cloves or pepper

Aluminum foil

6" (15cm) of 16- or 18-gauge copper wire

Driftwood

Acrylic paints: coral, blue, brown, black and white

Matte medium or blending gel (for use with acrylic paints)

Paintbrush

Basic tools (page 12)

Pattern (page 123)

Seated, AnnaBelle is 4½" (11cm) tall. Standing, she would be 5½" (14cm) tall.

notes from Woodpecker Pete

Thimbles can be hats or bowls, metal bottle caps are platters and a milkweed pod is a tiny baby cradle. If you aren't sure if an item is oven safe, test it by placing it on a piece of aluminum foil in a preheated, empty oven and baking it for 30 minutes. Check the oven frequently. If the item doesn't scorch or burn, then it's probably safe to bake along with your clay character.

1 Mark the center of a 6" (15cm) wire. Bend the wire at the mark, then twist the wire ends to form two $^3/_4$" (19mm) tall egg-shaped loops. Lay the wires over the pattern on page 123, adjusting the wires as necessary to match the pattern. Wrap 3" (8cm) foil strips around the wires to fill out the body form. Fit a small foil egg inside the head armature, wrapping the egg with more strips of foil to hold it in place.

2 Cover the body with a sheet of flesh-colored clay $^1/_8$" (3mm) thick. Smooth the clay and seams. For breasts, form two $^1/_2$" (13mm) balls into short cone shapes, then press them to the front of the body, blending the top edge of the cones into the body. For the head, roll a $^1/_2$" (13mm) ball for the back and a $^5/_8$" (16,m) egg for the front. Flatten them and cover the head, smoothing the seams. Use a rounded tool to press in the eye sockets. Position the body so that it will fit on the driftwood, then bake the body (not the driftwood), following the directions on the package of clay.

3 Cover the baked head with a layer of clay $^1/_8$" (3mm) thick. Mark the positions of the facial features. To determine the size needed for each feature, make the shape, using flesh-colored clay, and test it on the face. Adjust the size as needed: *Forehead*: a rope, flattened into a rectangle, with indentations for brow bones; *Nose*: a teardrop, pressed into a triangular cone; *Cheeks*: two teardrops, flattened and turned slightly; *Lips*: two short, flattened cones with one thicker edge; *Chin*: a short, flattened cone; *Ears*: two flattened teardrops, with indentations pressed into one side; *Eyelids*: two flattened footballs.

4 Place the eyes on the face, then fit the features on the face, trimming the pieces so that there is little or no overlap. Try to keep the features small to create a feminine face. Blend the seams by first smudging the edges, then rolling them with a needle tool to smooth. Add or remove small pieces of clay, as needed, to form and fill out the features.

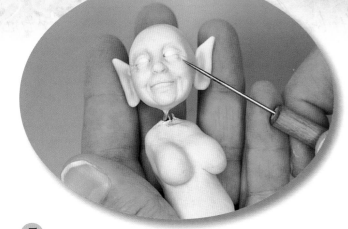

5 Add prebaked white clay eyeballs to the eye sockets. Lay half-moon eyelids over the eyes. Do a final blending and shaping of the features, using a clay brush for the final smoothing. Press on the ears and blend the seams. Add character details such as wrinkles around the eyes and mouth. If you wish to change the tilt or direction of the head, use flat-nosed pliers to bend the neck wires. Once the head is positioned, press flesh-colored clay for the neck over the wire, blending the seams and smoothing the clay.

6 For each leg, roll a 7/8" (22mm) ball of beige-mix clay. Mix a little paprika and ground cloves or pepper to give the clay a tweedy look. Roll each leg into a long, tapered rope with a quick turn at the knee. Shape the calf. For shoes, roll two 5/8" (16mm) balls of brown clay. Mix a little pepper or cloves and a small amount of beige-mix clay to lighten the color. Roll the shoes into long egg shapes. Flatten the egg slightly, then pinch the small end to form a heel. Roll the toe to create a point. Use a blunt tool to hollow out space for the leg to fit in the shoe.

7 Press the legs into the shoes and pinch the back of each shoe slightly to firmly hold each leg in place. Use your finger to flatten the inside edge of each upper thigh, then press the legs on the body. Position Annabelle Mae on the driftwood and bake both for 20 minutes, following the directions on the package of clay. Let the clay cool

8 Flatten the skirt clay to a sheet 1/16" (2mm) thick, then use the pattern on page 123 to cut out the skirt. Flatten the edges of the skirt, then tear away the bottom to create an uneven edge. Drape the skirt around your fingers, overlapping and sealing the seam. Fit the skirt over the head and into place at the waist. Shape the gathers with your fingers and a needle tool.

9 For the shirt, mix a 1 1/8" (28mm) ball of beige-mix clay with a tiny bit of paprika and cloves. For the sleeves, roll two 3/4" (19mm) balls, then roll the balls into 1 3/4" (4cm) ropes. Use this clay and the pattern on page 123 to cut out two shirt fronts, two cuffs and one back from a sheet of clay 1/16" (2mm) thick. For the vest, mix a 1" (25mm) ball of beige-mix clay with a small amount of paprika and cloves. Flatten the clay, then use the pattern on page 123 to cut out one vest piece and two sleeve caps.

10 Press the shirt back in place, trimming or stretching it to fit. Lay the shirt fronts in place, starting on the left side. Trim the shoulder seams. To shape the sleeves, make a soft bend at the elbows, then use a blunt tool to hollow out sleeves to the elbows. Make hands using the basic directions on page 20, but keep them only 3/4" (19mm) long. Cut finger lines, then carefully separate the fingers. Roll and pat the ends of the fingers until smooth. Reposition the fingers.

11 Wrap the cuffs around the wrists, then press the hands into the sleeves. Press the sleeves to the shoulders. Press an acorn cap in the lap, then position the hands around the cap. Brush a small amount of liquid polymer clay on the palms to help hold the cap in place. Add small brown buttons to the front of the vest, using the same brown clay used for the shoes. Press small pleats into one edge of each sleeve cap. Press each pleated edge against each shoulder of the vest with the seam on the inside. Flatten each edge with a needle tool. Flip the sleeve caps down over the top of each sleeve. Use a needle tool and a brush to adjust the pleats.

12 For hair, mix a 3/4" (19mm) ball of brown, a 5/8" (16mm) ball of gold, a 7/8" (22mm) ball of translucent and a 1/2" (13mm) ball of red. Mix until the clay is softly striped, then flatten it to a sheet 1/16" (2mm) thick. Use a knife to cut short fringes into the sheet. Separate the pieces with your fingers, then press the hair to the head, starting at the back. Press all the pieces together on top of the head, using a needle tool to press lines toward the center part. To finish, bake according to the directions on the package of clay. Let the clay cool. Paint the eyes following the directions on page 23.

a closet full of hats

*O*n some days, AnnaBelle Mae chooses to wear a hat that might belong to a free-spirit leprechaun. On other days, she dresses like an elf who loves to perform and tell stories. Changing hats is one way to quickly change the identity of a character. Is it an elf, a gnome, a pixie, a leprechaun? Often times it is the hat that tells us who a character is.

To fit a hat on a character you've already baked, use a crumpled foil hat form. Form the foil so it resembles the size and shape of the top of the character's head. Fit the clay hat onto the clay head, adjusting it as necessary, then remove it and place it on the foil hat form to bake.

Storyteller hat
To make the hat, mix together a $1^1/8$" (28mm) ball of translucent clay with rubbed sage. Flatten the clay to a sheet $^1/16$" (2mm) thick. Cut a rectangle that is $3^1/4$" x $1^3/4$" (8cm x 4cm). Fold one long side in half and overlap the edges. Roll over the edge of the unseamed side to make a brim. Tuck two clay leaves under the brim. Add a piece of grape vine or a wire that is curled to look like a vine. Press three red clay berries on the leaves. After baking, gloss the berries with polymer clay lacquer.

Pixie hat
To make the hat, mix together a 1" (25mm) ball of translucent clay with ground cloves. Make the hat the same as Olaf's hat (page 80), except make it shorter, then rip the edges to make them uneven. For the feathers, mix a $^1/4$" (6mm) ball of translucent clay with paprika and another with a tiny pinch of turmeric. For the leaves, mix together $^1/4$" (6mm) balls of green and translucent clay. Shape and flatten the leaves and feathers, then make lines with a knife, or press them with a real leaf.

Sweet William
the flower baby

Shhh. Work quietly as you pull the weeds from amongst the poppies. Sweet William is sleeping. Where, you might ask? Well, right there. Don't you see him? Cradled gently in the center of that lowest blossom? Peek carefully if you must, but don't touch. The elves have placed him there for safekeeping while they go about their daily chores. He's safe, you know, for the thistles are standing guard and the blackbirds will send a warning if you get too close.

Just imagine what it's like to be rocked to sleep in a cradle made of flower petals, kissed by the sun, caressed by warm breezes, and bathed in the scents of heather and sage. The Faerie Folk know how it feels, because most all of them begin life this way. Perhaps that's why the Faerie Folk are quick to break into song or dance. Once you've been cradled by flowers, your soul can never be earthbound again.

Use the instructions on page 95 to create a push mold to make several babies, one to place in the silk flower centerpiece and another to add to the wreath that hangs by the front door. No one else needs to see them. As long as you know they are there, that's enough. It can be a secret just between you and the fairies.

notes from Woodpecker Pete

Proportions are very important, as visual clues tell us the approximate age of people—even of elves and fairies. The baby's head is a fourth of its total length. Other clues tell us that this is a very young child. The eyes are below the half-line of the face, which makes the forehead quite large. The hands and feet are small, and the body is narrow, not much wider than the head at any point.

materials

Polymer clay: 2 ounces (57 grams) or less of beige, caramel, translucent, leaf green, white, dark brown, red, yellow, green and gold

Color recipes:
- For the flesh, mix 1 ounce (28 grams) of beige with $1/4$ ounce (7 grams) of caramel
- For the clothing, mix a $1/2$" (13mm) ball of white clay, a 1" (25mm) ball of translucent, a $1/2$" (13mm) ball of green clay and a little paprika
- For the eyes, use two prebaked $3/16$" (5mm) white clay balls

Paprika

Yellow string

5" (13cm) of 18- or 20-gauge copper wire

6" (15cm) of 28- or 32-gauge copper wire

2" (5cm) wide strip of cardboard

Aluminum foil

Acrylic paints: brown, coral, back and white

Matte medium or blending gel

Paintbrush

Baby powder or cornstarch

Pasta machine

Basic tools (page 12)

Patterns (page 124)

Optional: Brayer or clay roller, leaves

If the legs were stretched out, this baby would be $3^3/8$" (9cm) tall. The flower is 5" (13cm) long and $3^1/2$" (9cm) wide.

1 Mark the center of a 5" (13cm) wire. Bend the wire at the mark, then twist it to form a ½" (13mm) tall, egg-shaped loop for the head. Using flat-nosed pliers, twist the wires once at the neck. Curve the wire into a 1" (3cm) loop, overlapping the ends and wrapping them with wire to secure. Check the armature against the pattern on page 124, and make adjustments as necessary. Tear off a ½" (13mm) strip of aluminum foil. Insert folded foil into the head loop, then wrap it around the head. Roll, then slightly flatten, two ½" (13mm) balls of flesh-colored clay. Position the clay on the head, then blend the seams. Add a ⅜" (9mm) ball of clay to build up the top of the head and a ¼" (6mm) ball to build up the chin.

2 Mark a center line on the head, then draw the facial features with a needle tool, being sure that the eyes are below the line. Use a rounded tool to create the eye sockets. Then shape each facial feature using flesh-colored clay: *Forehead*: one ¼" (6mm) ball of clay, flattened into a rectangle with indentations for the eye sockets; *Nose*: one ⅛" (3mm) ball of clay, shaped into a teardrop, then into a triangular cone; *Cheeks*: two ¼" (6mm) balls of clay, flattened into teardrops, with indentations for the eye sockets; *Lips*: two ⅛" (3mm) balls of clay, shaped into flattened footballs; *Chin*: one ⅛" (3mm) ball of clay, flattened into a half circle; *Ears*: two 3/16" (5mm) balls of clay, shaped into flattened teardrops, with indentations pressed into one side.

Fit the features, except the ears and eyes, in place on the face. Trim the features so there is little or no overlap.

notes from Woodpecker Pete

Firm clay works best for this project, as you will be adding lots of detail. If clay is too soft, leach out some of the plasticizer by laying thin sheets of the clay between pieces of white paper. It shouldn't take long for you to notice results.

3 Blend the cheeks into the side of the head. Draw a vertical line along the profile of the head. Blend the seam lines, then add or remove small pieces of clay as needed to form and fill out the features. On the side of the head, draw ears behind the line and between the bottoms of the eyes and the bottom of the lips.

4 Place the prebaked white clay eyeballs in the eye sockets. Smooth the upper cheek areas. Shape the nose and press in the nostrils. Add tiny flattened football shapes for the lower lids and a flattened half-circle for the upper lid. Add a small football shape for the fleshy area above the eyes. Do final blending and shaping of the features. Use a clay brush for the final smoothing. If the skin isn't smooth, the Flower Baby will look like an aging elf!

5 Add the ears. The bigger ears add the touch of Faerie to this project. Check the profile. You might want to add more clay to the forehead, as babies often have protruding foreheads. Bake the head for 20 minutes, following the directions on the package of clay.

6 Fill the body armature loop with foil, being sure that the body still fits within the pattern. Cover the body with a layer of flesh-colored clay. Smooth the seams and shape the body. Check the position of the head. If you wish to change the tilt or direction of the head, use flat-nosed pliers to bend the neck wires. Once the head is positioned, blend the neck area. Shape the chest and belly by rolling a knitting needle along wrinkled areas. Blend and smooth the clay. Press in a belly button. It won't show, but every baby needs a belly button.

notes

If you would like to make a mold of the Flower Baby's face, you should do so after step 5. See page 95 for more information on creating and using molds.

7 Shape the backside just enough to give form to the body and help fill the shape beneath the clothing.

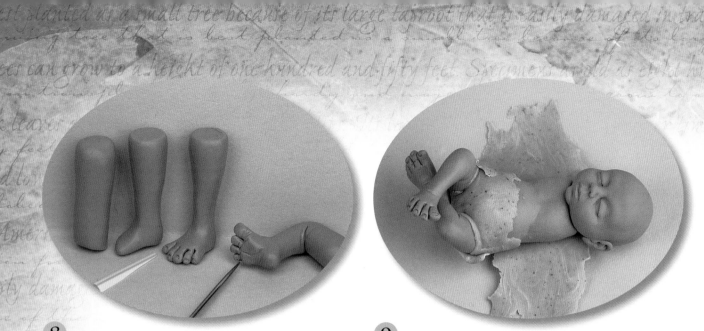

8 Make the legs, beginning with a ⁵⁄₈" (16mm) ball of flesh-colored clay for each leg. Roll the balls into 1" (3cm) ropes. Make the feet ⁷⁄₁₆" (11mm) long. Shape the ankles and bend the knees. Trim or stretch each leg to 1" (25mm) long.

9 Press the legs on the baby. Flatten the clay used for clothing to a sheet ¹⁄₁₆" (2mm) thick. Cut a diaper-shaped piece of clay to fit between the legs and around the waist. Tear the edges. Position it on the body, stretching the clay if needed. Ruffle the edges by rolling them upward with your fingers. For a shirt, cut a 2" x 1" (5cm x 3cm) rectangle from the sheet of flattened clay. Tear the edges, then wrap it around the baby, tearing away the excess clay. Ruffle the edges as you did for the diaper.

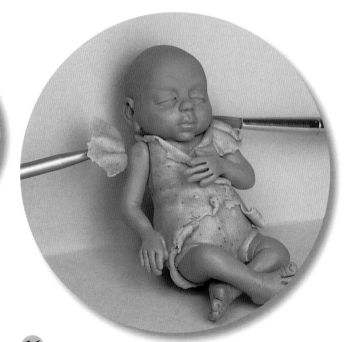

10 To make the arms, roll a ¹⁄₂" (13mm) ball of clay for each arm into 1" (25mm) ropes. Roll the wrists, making hands that are ¹⁄₄" (6mm) long. Flatten the ends of the hands slightly, then cut lines for the fingers. Smooth the thumbs. Carefully separate the fingers, then roll the end of each finger, being careful not to stretch the clay. Use a needle tool and a piece of drinking straw (step 3, page 20) to add detail to the fingers and fingernails. Bend the arms to form elbows. Use the back of a knife or the side of a needle to add wrinkle lines at the elbows.

11 Press the arms over the shirt at the shoulders. Add a short strip of clothing clay over the tops of the arms to camouflage the seams. Press the clay in place with a brush, lifting the edges and tucking in the corners. Do a final positioning of the arms and legs. Bake the figure for 20 minutes, following the directions on the package of clay. Let the clay cool.

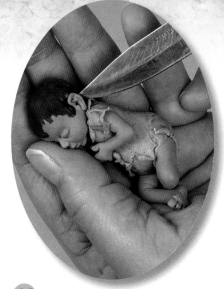

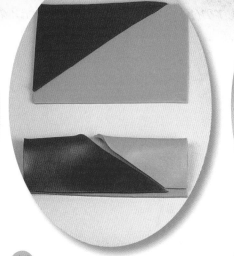

12 Soften a ¹/₄" (6mm) ball of dark brown clay. Press the clay onto the head, following the hairline, until the clay is so thin the scalp shows through in some places. Trim away clay that is too thick. Use a knife to cut hair lines along the edges. Use your finger to soften the lines. Bake the figure for 20 minutes, following the directions on the package of clay. When cool, brush the skin with a watery application of brown paint. Leave no dark lines behind. Paint in very fine eyebrows. For blush at the knees, elbows, nose, fingers, toes and cheeks, mix a tiny bit of coral paint into matte medium or blending gel. Let the paint dry.

13 To create the flower, you'll need to make a Skinner blend. Begin by flattening both red and yellow clay on the thickest setting of the pasta machine. Cut a 4" x 3" (10cm x 8cm) rectangle of each color. Cut the rectangles into triangles using the pattern on page 124. Note that the red clay is a smaller triangle, and that the top of the yellow triangle is cut flat. Combine the triangles to create a mixed-color rectangle, then fold the rectangle in half so that each side, with like colors, folds on top of itself. Remember this position, as you will be repeating this step of folding and rolling approximately ten to twenty times.

14 Place the folded rectangle in the pasta machine with the folded side against the rollers. Be sure that the sheet is lined up straight against the rollers. Roll the rectangle through the machine. Repeat, folding the sheet so that the like colors touch, then rolling it through the pasta machine until the clay is blended in a graduated pattern. At first the colors will form a marble blend, then stripes. Finally it will blend into a gradual shift of colors. Notice that one side is still yellow. That is because, in the original triangles, the red clay did not reach the upper right corner.

15 Fold the clay again so that like colors touch. Place the clay against the rollers of the pasta machine so the fold is on the side, not against the rollers, and roll. Place the clay back on the rollers, rolling the sheet through in the same direction, creating a long, thin clay strip. Fold the long clay strip back and forth in an accordion pleat. Press the resulting clay block firmly together with the palm of your hand, or compress it with a brayer or clay roller.

16 To make flower petals, use a very sharp polymer clay blade to cut six slices $1/8"$ to $3/16"$ (3mm to 5mm) thick from the compressed block of clay. Pinch the yellow side of each slice against itself, then press and shape the slice into a petal shape with your fingers. Flatten the petal between your hands to a sheet $1/16"$ (2mm) thick at the darkest edges, slightly thicker in the center and at the yellow edge. Ruffle the edges by stretching the clay carefully. Place three petals together, with the yellow centers pressed together.

17 Create a second grouping of three petals. Press one group over the other so that the petals alternate. To make the yellow center of the flower, wrap yellow crochet cotton approximately thirty times around a 2" (5cm) strip of cardboard. Slip the loops off the cardboard, then wrap the center with another piece of string. Cut the loops on both sides. Press this into the center of the flower. Press a $1/4"$ (6mm) ball of brown clay over the center to hold the string in place. To make leaves, start with $7/8"$ (22mm) balls of leaf green clay. Shape the balls into teardrops, then into leaf shapes. To make leaf veins, press the clay onto a real leaf. Finally, press the leaves under the petals.

18 Press the finished baby in the flower. To prevent sticking, apply baby powder or cornstarch under the baby. Apply only until silky, brushing away any white residue. Curl the petal edges around the baby. Prop the petals. Place paper towels between the petals and supports to prevent shiny spots. Remove the baby from the flower. To keep the center of the flower open, use a rolled piece of paper towel to duplicate the baby's shape. To make the flower very sturdy, bake the flower for the longest and hottest time recommended on the package of clay.

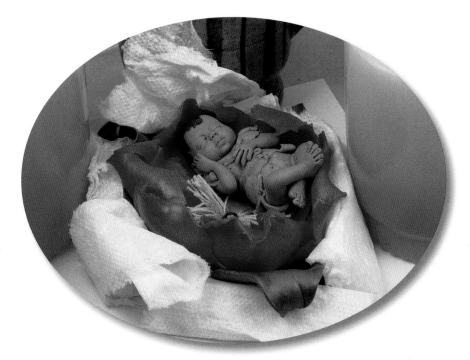

life beyond
the flowers

*t*he small baby can fit into more than just the flower. Adding the baby to a scene with other characters in the book can create whole new stories for your characters. Humboldt the Troll, for example, doesn't seem nearly so fearsome as he guards the baby sleeping in a nest.

Creating more baby characters is easy when you use your own original push molds. Once you have a push mold, it's easy to create duplicate faces, so you don't have to worry so much about wrecking a face. One mold can yield a whole clan of characters. Stretch the face lengthwise, push the sides together or stretch them out. In fact, the stretching, squeezing, flattening, adding ears and altering of the push mold faces is half of the fun.

For information on making Humboldt the Troll, turn to page 60.

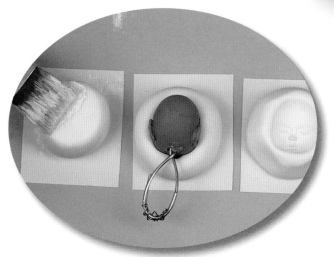

Creating a mold

Begin with a ball of very soft polymer clay. The ball should be about twice the width and depth of the face that you wish to mold. Brush the clay with baby powder or cornstarch, then smooth away extra powder. Pack the nostrils of a finished, baked head with clay, then press the finished head into the ball of clay, stopping before you reach the ears. Pull the finished head straight out from the mold. Bake the mold for 45 minutes, following the directions on the package of clay.

Using the mold

Brush the mold with baby powder or cornstarch. Roll clay into a short cone shape. Position the tip of the cone in the nose of the mold, then press firmly. Try not to overfill the mold by using too much clay. Use your finger to separate the edge of the face from the sides of the mold. Press a second piece of clay to the back of the face. Lift the face straight out from the mold.

Phoebe Lu
the playful fairy

hoebe Lu isn't a tiny fairy like the ones who hide in the hyacinths, and she isn't a tall, graceful fairy like those who dance away with the hearts of men. No, she isn't one of those. What she most likes to be called is a playful fairy, for she is one who plays. Oh, she does more than just play—she sweeps the mossy carpet free of fallen leaves and trims shriveled blossoms from the daffodils. But she never calls it work. She chooses to see everything she does as play.

Long ago, she decided that she wouldn't use words that made her sad. And the word *work* was that kind of word. So she just stopped using it to describe anything that she did. The other fairies get jealous that all Phoebe Lu does is play, but she just laughs and smiles as she mends her dress or stirs tiny berries into jam. How lucky can she be to be a fairy whose play is never done?

It might be fun to make a playful fairy to sit by your computer or your mop bucket or the kitchen sink. Who knows, even the worst job might become play with the help of a Playful Fairy.

notes from Woodpecker Pete

The face for Phoebe Lu comes from a face mold that you make from Sweet William on page 88, following the directions on page 95. If you didn't make that character, you can still make Phoebe Lu. Just follow the basic directions for making Sweet William's face, but build it on Phoebe Lu's armature. Then alter the face by making it narrower. Leave the eyes open and pull the center of the mouth down into a funny grin. Be sure to make a mold of the finished face so that you can easily make a playmate for Phoebe Lu.

materials

Polymer clay: 2 ounces or less of beige, caramel, white, leaf green, black, blue and light turquoise

Color recipes:
- For the flesh, mix 1 ounce (28 grams) of beige and $^1/_4$ ounce (7 grams) of caramel
- For the eyes, use two prebaked, $^3/_{16}$" (5mm) white clay balls

Push mold made from the Flower Baby face on page 88 (Directions for making the mold are on page 95.)

Flat rock

Aluminum foil

6" (15cm) of 18- or 20-gauge copper wire

3" (8cm) of 24- to 32-gauge white wire

6 " (15cm) of 28- or 32-gauge copper wire

White cardstock

Acrylic paints: Black, white, brown, coral and blue

Matte medium or blending gel (for use with acrylic paints)

Drill

Pasta machine

Sponge

Paintbrush

Craft glue

Basic tools (page 12)

Pattern (page 124)

Phoebe Lu is 3" (8cm) tall when seated, and would be 5" (13cm) tall when standing.

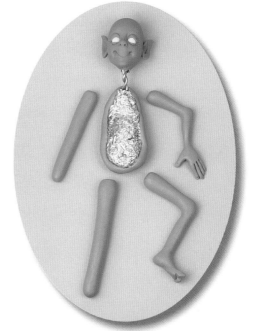

1 Mark the center of the 6" (15cm) wire. Bend the wire at the mark, then twist at the bend to form a $^5/_8$" (16mm) tall egg-shaped loop for the head. Twist the wires three times at the neck. Following the pattern on page 124, curve the wire ends into a 1$^1/_4$" (3cm) long, narrow loop. Overlap the wire ends, then secure them with the smaller wire. Tear off a $^1/_2$" (13mm) strip of aluminum foil. Insert the bunched foil into the head loop, then wrap more foil to secure. Press the foil front slightly flat. Using flesh-colored clay, slightly flatten a $^1/_2$" (13mm) ball for the back of the head and a $^3/_8$" (9mm) ball for the front. Position the clay on the head, then blend the seams with your fingers. Using a $^9/_{16}$" (14mm) ball of clay, make a face from a push mold, following the directions on page 95.

2 Press the face on the armature. Blend the side seams, using a knitting needle to blend the clay under the chin. Shape the chin area, adding more clay to form a protruding chin. Use a rounded tool to create eye sockets. Smooth the clay around the eyes to remove the closed eyelid lines. Make the nose longer by pulling the clay down and toward the center of the nose, adding more clay if needed. Create nostrils, then press the prebaked eyes into the eye sockets. Mark the corners of the eyes.

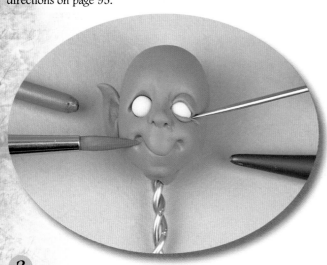

3 Add tiny flattened football shapes for the lower lids and larger ones for the upper lids. Use a sharp needle tool to create smile lines at the corners of the eyes. Use $^3/_{16}$" (5mm) balls of flesh-colored clay rolled into teardrop shapes, then flattened, for the ears. On a fairy, the ear shape can be exaggerated. Smooth the face, using a clay brush for the final details. Bake the head for 20 minutes, following the directions on the package of clay. Let the clay cool.

4 Use pliers to bend the neck into position, then fill the body armature with foil. Wrap with more foil to secure. Cover the front and back with flesh-colored clay. Begin the arms with $^9/_{16}$" (14mm) balls of clay rolled into ropes 1$^3/_4$" (4cm) long. Roll each wrist to create a hand that is $^1/_2$" (1cm) long. Bend each arm at the midpoint to create an elbow. Each finished arm, including the hand, is approximately 2" (5cm) long. Begin the legs with $^5/_8$" (16mm) balls of clay that are rolled into 2$^1/_4$" (6cm) ropes. Bend each leg to create a $^5/_8$" (16mm) foot. Create the knees with quick turns. The finished legs are 2$^1/_4$" (6cm) long. See pages 20-21 for more information on sculpting hands and feet.

5 Smooth and shape the body. Add clay to the neck. Notice that the fairy's neck is much longer than the Flower Baby's. Press the legs in place, smoothing the clay and adjusting the legs if needed. Position the fairy on the rock, making more adjustments as needed.

6 Create a Skinner blend for the fairy's clothing. Flatten pieces of white, blue and light turquoise clay at a medium setting on a pasta machine. Cut a 4" x 3" (10cm x 8cm) rectangle from white clay. Using the pattern on page 124, lay blue, white and turquoise clay on the white rectangle, then follow the directions for creating a Skinner blend on page 93. Cut ten to twenty 1" to 2" (3cm to 5cm) long petal shapes from the Skinner blend.

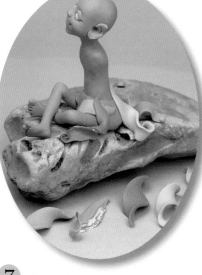

7 Flatten the petal edges by pressing and rolling them between the palms of your hands. Twist and curl the petals carefully. Press the clay on the fairy's bottom, then press the curled petals to her waist, so they droop over her legs.

8 Wrap a strip of Skinner blend clay around the chest and back of the fairy. Rip the edges to give a loose feeling to the clothing. Use a knitting needle to blend the shirt into the skirt. Use a brush to position petals that make up the skirt.

9 Position the arms, hands, wrists and elbows as needed. Make the same pose with your own hands to see if the position is natural. Press the arms in place on the figure. To cover the shoulder seams, cut two narrow strips of Skinner blend clay, then rip the edges. Press the strips in place, then add a Skinner blend clay button to the front of the strips.

10 For the hair, flatten a $^{3}/_{8}$" (9mm) ball of black clay and press it on top of the head. Smooth the clay down to just above the hairline. Cut skinny fringes approximately 1" (3cm) long from a flattened strip of black clay. Twist each fringe of hair, then press it to the head, beginning at the back and sides. Use a needle tool to add hair in hard-to-reach areas.

11 Press a needle tool around the head to create space for the headband. Roll leaf green clay into a thin rope and lay it in the space. Add tiny leaves made from flattened teardrop shapes and ribbons cut from the Skinner blend. Bake the fairy in an oven, following the directions on the package of clay. Because there are many very fragile pieces on the fairy, bake at the hottest temperature and for the longest time recommended on package. Brush the cooled fairy with a watery application of brown paint. Don't leave any dark lines. Paint the eyes and eyebrows following the directions on page 23. For blush at the knees, elbows, nose, fingers, toes and cheeks, mix a tiny bit of coral paint into matte medium or blending gel and then apply it to these areas. Let dry.

12 To make wings, dip a damp sponge into water-thinned blue paint. Wring the sponge until it is nearly dry, then dab it onto both sides of a piece of cardstock. Let the cardstock dry. Cut out the wings, using the pattern on page 124. Overlap the wings slightly, then glue them together at the center. Glue the white wire over the center. Let dry. Cut two small squares of painted paper and glue one on each side of the wings to cover the wire and make a sturdier center section. Let them dry. Curl the wings slightly by curving the paper along the center line of the wings.

13 Twist the wire ends together. Use a small drill to create a hole in the center back of the fairy. Drill at an angle, being careful not to drill through the fairy. Trim the wire to fit in the hole, then glue the wire in the hole to hold the wings in place. The wings may also be left unglued so that they can be removed for packing or shipping.

a fairy's best friend

*d*affodil, Phoebe Lu's sister, isn't really fond of frogs, but she is a big believer in possibilites. One never knows where a prince might be hiding!

To give her a kissing expression, her mouth was pushed forward a bit from both sides, and her chin was pushed back. Her position is similar to Phoebe's, but she leans forward more. She can look the frog right in the eye, then choose whether to kiss him or not.

Daffodil's hair is a mix of light beige, gold and translucent clay. The yellow for her dress is made using a Skinner blend of white and yellow clay. You can find information on making the flower on pages 93-94.

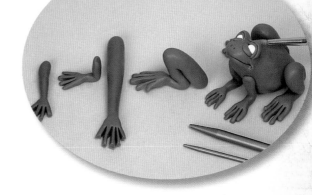

Sculpting the frog

1 Begin with a 1¹/₂" (4cm) long foil football. Press it against your work surface so the bottom is flat and one end tips up. Flatten a 1" (3cm) ball of green clay and cover the football. Smooth the clay into the shape of a frog body, with a slight indentation to mark the head. Press ³/₁₆" (5mm) prebaked white clay eyeballs in the face. Add eyelids. Add a half-circle of clay over the top of each eye. Blend these pieces into the back of the head.

2 To make legs, roll two ¹/₂" (13mm) balls for the front legs and ³/₄" (19mm) balls for the back legs. Begin each as you would begin hands, but take into consideration that the front legs only have four toes. Bend the front legs once and the back legs twice. Press the legs to the body. Smooth and blend the seams. Bake the frog for 20 minutes. Let the clay cool, then paint the frog's eyes.

magical
Mischievous Marvin
the trickster elf

If you watch a forest path at just the right time, you might see the Faerie Folk pass by on their way to the Midsummer Ball. As they glide by, it's easy to recognize that some, such as Olaf the Wise, are gnomes, and that others, such Humboldt, are trolls. But finding a label for Magical Mischievous Marvin is not so easy a task. Perhaps you have seen him on other occasions, but he is such a master of disguise that you can never tell exactly who, or what, he is.

There is the matter of his disguises—of which he has several. If his tall, pointed hat makes him look like a gnome, does the very same hat, tilted and falling to the side, turn him into an elf? If he were to appear in his elf hat, but wearing the troll mask, would you think "troll" when you saw him pass by, or could you tell that he was just a trickster, playing with your eyes?

Make some mischievous magic yourself by creating several hats and masks for Magical Mischievous Marvin. When you do so, your little clay figure becomes not only a beautiful piece of art, but also an interactive character who involves both the maker and the viewer in his story.

materials

Polymer clay: 6 ounces (170 grams) of beige and 2 ounces (57 grams) or less of the following colors: caramel, leaf green, light flesh, light turquoise, gold, ultramarine blue, dark brown and white

Color recipes:
- For the skin, mix 1$\frac{1}{2}$ ounces (43 grams) of light flesh-colored clay with $\frac{1}{2}$ ounce (14 grams) of caramel clay
- For the bench, mix 2 ounces (57 grams) of white clay with bits of leftover brown or muddied clays

11" (28cm) of 18-gauge wire (soft metal rods and thin or medium brass will also work)

Aluminum foil

Acrylic paints: brown, coral, blue, black and white

Matte medium or blending gel (for use with acrylic paints)

Paintbrush

Basic tools (page 12)

Patterns (page 125)

Magical Mischievous Marvin is 5$\frac{1}{2}$" (14cm) tall, and, without his hats, would be 7$\frac{1}{2}$" (19cm) tall standing.

notes from Woodpecker Pete

To make the muted pastel colors of Marvin's many-colored clothes, mix equal parts of light beige and the main color for the darker tones. For lighter tones, mix three parts light beige with one part of the main color. Since the intensity of the color varies between brands of clay, mix a small amount at first. You can then adjust your recipe and easily make more as needed in the future.

1 Follow the directions in step 1 on page 76 to create the body armature for Marvin. Create only the top half of the armature, narrowing the shoulders and hips. Follow the directions for making Olaf's face on pages 76-77, using slightly smaller balls of clay. Bend the neck wire to position the head. Add clay to the neck, blending it into both the head and the body. For the bench, crumple foil into a block that is 1¼" (31mm) thick, 1¾" (4cm) wide and 2½" (6cm) tall. Press the foil block against your work surface, making it very firm and the bottom side flat. Flatten the clay for the bench to a sheet ⅛" (3mm) thick. Cover the foil, then add texture with a piece of fabric. Bake the bench, the body armature and the head, following the instructions on the package of clay.

2 Roll three 1" (25mm) balls from gold clay. Flatten one ball to a sheet ⅛" (3mm) thick. Set the body armature in the center of the flattened circle, then press the sides up to cover the bottom third of the armature. Smooth the clay. Roll the other two balls of clay into tapered, 2" (5cm) ropes. Insert a rounded tool halfway into the pant legs and hollow them to the knees. Bend and shape the knees. Press your thumb along one edge of the pantleg top to make a groove for the body. Fold a ⅛" (3mm) edge in along each of the pantlegs.

3 For the shoes, roll two ⅞" (22mm) balls of blue clay into 2½" (6cm) tapered teardrop shapes. Make a soft bend ¾" (19mm) from the thicker end. Use a rounded tool to hollow out the shoes. Form the heels. For each leg, roll a ⅞" (22mm) ball of pale green clay into a 2" (5cm) teardrop. Insert each leg into a shoe. Use a knitting needle to press a groove around the ankle. To make a striped accent, flatten a small piece of both pale beige and blue clay to a sheet ⅛" (3mm) thick. Cut a 1" x ½" (25mm x 13mm) rectangle from each sheet, then stack the rectangles. This is a striped stack. Using a sharp clay blade, cut the stack in half. Make a total of eight layers this way. Cut a ⅛" (3mm) piece of striped clay to place around each ankle.

4 Roll up the tips of the shoes. Insert the legs into the pant legs. Shape the knees, making sure the legs are secure. Make wrinkle lines in the pants with the back of a knife. Press the body to the top of the pant legs. Blend the tops of the legs into the sides and back of the body. Set the body on the stone bench you made in step 1, making sure the bench is stable and the body balanced. You should still be able to remove the body from the bench.

5 Mix a variety of tones of blue, green, turquoise and beige for the jacket, shirt and vest. Use other colors for the pockets, buttons and belt. For this figure, a second striped stack was made using beige and rust-colored clays. Flatten each piece to a sheet $1/8$" (3mm) thick. Use the patterns on page 123 to make the vest and shirt, cutting two pieces for each and pressing them together. Add texture with a paper towel, then add the buttons and pockets. Create a jacket with a 6" x 3" (15cm x 8cm) rectangle. Place a small piece of paper towel under the pockets, then add the pockets and clay buttons. Cut buttonholes. Fold over the top corners and press a pleat in the back. Make stitch marks around the pockets with a sharp needle. Add a belt to the back of the jacket.

6 Fit the shirt to the neck. Pull the edges of the shirt toward the shoulder. Add a vest over the shirt. Finally, add the coat over the shirt and vest. Make sure there is enough clay at the shoulders of the shirt to hold the sleeves securely, without putting too much stress on the back of the jacket.

7 Begin the hands with a $3/4$" (19mm) ball of flesh-colored clay rolled into a $1 1/2$" (38mm) rope. Finish the hands using the steps on page 20. Each finished hand is $1 1/4$" (31mm) long. Wrap each wrist with a flat strip of green-toned clay to resemble cuffs. For added embellishment, make a striped stack from pale green and beige clay, then add slices to the cuffs before wrapping them around the wrists. Begin the sleeves with $7/8$" (22mm) balls of blue-toned clay rolled into $1 3/4$" (44mm) tapered ropes. Hollow out the tapered ends to the elbows. Press the hands in the sleeves, trimming the arms as needed to fit. Press the arms to the shoulders, adding both at the same time. Position the hands. You will need to support the arms and hands while baking.

8 Cut a 6" x 1" (15cm x 3cm) strip from a $^1/_8$" (3mm) thick sheet of pale green clay. To make striped clay from scraps of clay, gather together coordinating colors and roll the clay into a rope. Twist by rotating the ends in opposite directions. Cut small pieces of plain, striped and patterned clay flattened to a sheet $^1/_{16}$" (2mm) thick, then use the pieces to cover the strip of pale green clay. Trim the edges and press them between your palms to bevel. Add texture with a paper towel. Wrap the scarf around the figure's neck, positioning the folds with a soft brush.

9 For the hair, flatten dark brown clay to a sheet $^1/_8$" (3mm) thick. Cut a 1" (3cm) strip, then use a knife to create a fringe. Add the strips to the head, following the hair line. Make sure the hair is flat. Use a small needle tool to create hair lines. Bake according to the directions on the package of clay. Let the clay cool, then paint and antique the face and hands. Dab blush made from a bit of coral paint mixed into matte medium or blending gel. Paint the eyes following the instructions on page 23.

notes

If necessary, press a hole into each side of the mask to use for attaching a string to help hold the mask in place when a character wears it.

10 Place a piece of foil over Marvin's face and nose. Build a half-mask over the foil, matching the eyes and nose of the mask and face. Carefully remove the foil and check the fit. Make adjustments as needed. Bake the mask for 30 minutes, following the directions on the package of clay. Support the mask with paper towels or aluminum foil. Make sure the cooled mask fits the face. If necessary, trim the high spots with a sharp blade.

11 Make a hat using a $^7/_8$" (22mm) ball of blue clay for the brim and a $^7/_8$" (22mm) ball of mixed gold and blue for the crown. Flatten the blue ball into a 2" (5cm) circle. Cut out a $^3/_4$" (19mm) hole in the center. Roll the mixed clay into a $1^1/_2$" (38mm) rope. Hollow out the center, leaving one end closed. Set the hollowed rope on the circle. Press the seams together. Stretch the opening in the hat until it fits loosely over Marvin's head and the mask. Add embellishments to the hat. Remove the hat to bake, supporting it with foil and paper towels. Bake for 30 minutes, following the instructions on the package of clay. Let the hat cool on the head and over the mask. If needed, trim the high spots inside the hat so that it fits.

a few tricks for marvin

$\mathcal{M}$arvin, like most tricksters out there, likes to involve others in his antics. He has so many tricks, it seems, that he has enough to go around. One way to share his fun with the other characters in this book is to see if one of his masks or hats will fit anyone else. You might try the half-mask on Drey Van Elm to see if he becomes more mysterious, or put the large mask from this page onto Woodpecker Pete to see if he starts acting like a troll. Just be sure that when you're done, all the hats and masks get returned to Marvin's care.

Marvin's mask

1 Cover the head and shoulders of the baked figure with two layers of foil. Press the foil tightly to the face. Flatten a $^7/_8$" (22mm) ball of flesh-colored clay into a $^1/_8$" (3mm) thick circle. Press this over Marvin's face, being careful not to rip the foil. Trim the clay just in front of the ears, under the chin and at the hairline. Press in the eye sockets and add unbaked white clay eyeballs, irises and pupils, following the directions on page 23. Add cheeks, lips and chin, just as you did when making the original Marvin face, but with exaggerated features using larger balls of clay.

2 Continue to sculpt, adding or removing clay as needed to create a very different face from Marvin's. Notice that one eyebrow is higher than the other, as is one side of the mouth. Brush on powder blush, blending it with a brush that is dampened with either liquid polymer clay or a clay softener liquid. Add hair, gluing it to the mask. When finished, bake the mask for 30 minutes, following the instructions on the package of clay.

Drey Van Elm
the elf king

When the Elf King enters the forest clearing, all idle chatter ceases. The tiny fairies stop gossiping, the gnomes stop telling stories and even the trolls stop mumbling and grumbling.

It's not that Drey Van Elm is fierce or cruel. He's not. It's more that there is an attitude about him that commands respect. Everything about him is straight and tall, even his inner determination and resolve. And every one of the Faerie Folk can sense it. No one tries to deceive the Elf King more than once. For he has a look of knowing in his eyes that registers amusement at minor deceptions, but grave disappointment at those of larger worth.

There are some who say Drey laughs and plays when his crown is removed and his staff is put down for the day, and I'm sure that it is true. But few have ever seen or heard it.

Make Drey Van Elm, then use the same directions to make an elf queen to stand beside him. Being the king can be a lonely thing, so to make a friend and equal for him would be grand. When you sculpt the queen's face and hands, make each of the features smaller than the king's so that she looks more feminine.

notes from Woodpecker Pete

Drey Van Elm is the tallest standing character in this book, even without his hats. To bake him safely, you'll need an oven or baking container that is at least 10" (25cm) tall.

materials

Polymer clay: 4 ounces (114 grams) each of purple and leaf green; 2 ounces (57 grams) or less of blue, brown, flesh color of your choice, silver, gold and white; 1 ounce (28 grams) of scrap polymer clay

Color recipes:
- For metallic purple, mix 4 ounces (114 grams) of purple clay with $^1/_2$ ounce (14 grams) of gold
- For metallic green, mix 4 ounces (114 grams) of leaf green with 1 ounce (28 grams) of gold
- For metallic blue, mix $^1/_2$ ounce (14 grams) of blue clay with a $^1/_2$" (13mm) ball of gold
- For the staff, mix a $^3/_4$" (19mm) ball of both brown and white clay until marbled
- For the off-white, mix 2 ounces (57 grams) of white clay with a $^3/_8$" (9mm) ball of gold, leaving the mix slightly streaked
- For the eyes, use two prebaked $^1/_8$" (3mm) white clay balls

Liquid polymer clay

6" (15cm), 9" (23cm), $3^3/_4$" (10cm) and two $1^1/_2$" (4cm) pieces of medium brass soft metal rod (by AMACO)

$1^1/_2$" (4cm) wide rock

Cardstock

Aluminum foil

Acrylic paints: brown, coral, blue, black and white

Matte medium or blending gel (for use with acrylic paints)

Sun push mold (by AMACO)

$^1/_4$" (6mm) leaf cutter

Fabric and leaves for texture

Paintbrush

Basic tools (page 12)

Drey Van Elm is 8" (20cm) tall. His head measures $1^1/_3$" (3cm) from tip of chin to top of head.

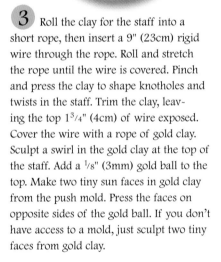

1 Crumple a 2' (61cm) sheet of foil around a small rock to create a loose, 6½" (17cm) tall, cone-shaped armature with the rock inside the base. Compress the base till it's 2" (5cm) wide. Flatten the top to 1" (25mm) across and ½" (13mm) thick. Fold a 6" (15cm) wire in half to form a ⅞" (22mm) tall loop in the center. Twist the loop, then bend the wire ends together. Insert the wire ends in the top of the foil armature so the neck and closed loop protrude. Indent the waist area 2¾" (7cm) from the top of the loop. Add more foil until the armature is firm. Smooth and shape the foil. Wrap a strip of foil through the wire loop, then cover the back of the head with a ¾" (19mm) ball of flesh-colored clay and the front with a ⅝" (16mm) ball rolled into an egg shape. Smooth the clay, then press in eye sockets just above the half-line mark.

2 Flatten a 1¼" (31mm) ball of scrap clay into a 5" (13cm) circle. Cover the bottom of the armature, pulling the excess clay up the sides and smoothing the creases. Flatten a 1" (25mm) ball of metallic purple clay into a 4" (100mm) circle and cover the scrap clay. For legs, roll two ⅞" (22mm) balls of metallic green clay into two 4" (100mm) long ropes. Bend over 1" (25mm) on the end of each to make a tapered, pointed shoe. Attach one leg to the right side of the figure. Cut half the foot from the other leg and attach the foot to the left side of the figure. Bake the armature for 30 minutes, following the directions on the package of clay. Let it cool.

3 Roll the clay for the staff into a short rope, then insert a 9" (23cm) rigid wire through the rope. Roll and stretch the rope until the wire is covered. Pinch and press the clay to shape knotholes and twists in the staff. Trim the clay, leaving the top 1¾" (4cm) of wire exposed. Cover the wire with a rope of gold clay. Sculpt a swirl in the gold clay at the top of the staff. Add a ⅛" (3mm) gold ball to the top. Make two tiny sun faces in gold clay from the push mold. Press the faces on opposite sides of the gold ball. If you don't have access to a mold, just sculpt two tiny faces from gold clay.

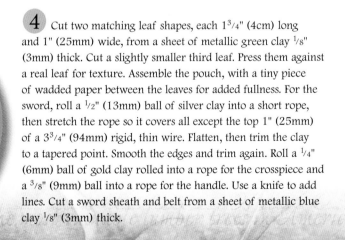

4 Cut two matching leaf shapes, each 1¾" (4cm) long and 1" (25mm) wide, from a sheet of metallic green clay ⅛" (3mm) thick. Cut a slightly smaller third leaf. Press them against a real leaf for texture. Assemble the pouch, with a tiny piece of wadded paper between the leaves for added fullness. For the sword, roll a ½" (13mm) ball of silver clay into a short rope, then stretch the rope so it covers all except the top 1" (25mm) of a 3¾" (94mm) rigid, thin wire. Flatten, then trim the clay to a tapered point. Smooth the edges and trim again. Roll a ¼" (6mm) ball of gold clay rolled into a rope for the crosspiece and a ⅜" (9mm) ball into a rope for the handle. Use a knife to add lines. Cut a sword sheath and belt from a sheet of metallic blue clay ⅛" (3mm) thick.

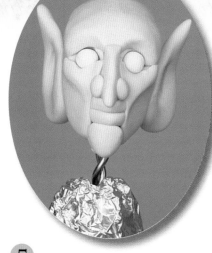

5 Smooth and shape the head, then use a needle tool to draw facial features. Give Drey a long nose and a narrow face. Roll and shape the features using flesh-colored clay: *Forehead*: 5/8" (16mm) ball of clay, flattened into a rectangle with indentations for the brows; *Nose*: 1/4" (6mm) ball of clay, shaped into a teardrop then a long, narrow cone; *Cheeks*: two 3/8" (9mm) balls of clay, shaped into flattened teardrops; *Lips*: two 3/16" (5mm) balls of clay, shaped into flattened triangles with one thicker edge; *Chin*: 3/8" (9mm) ball of clay, shaped into a flattened half-circle; *Ears*: two 1/2" (13mm) balls of clay, shaped into flattened teardrops. Lay the features over the face, starting in this order: bottom lip, top lip, nose, chin, cheeks, forehead, ears. Deepen the eye sockets with a rounded tool. Press your thumbs against each cheek to create high cheekbones and hollow centers. Add the eyes. A small ball of clay was added to both sides of the nose to create more distinctive nostrils.

6 Blend the seams and make adjustments. Shape the ears and add eyelids and wrinkle lines. Do a final smoothing and make adjustments to the head and neck positions. Add clay to fill out the neck. Bake the finished head, staff and sword for 20 minutes, following the directions on the package of clay. Let them cool.

7 Cut two angled pieces, each 6" (15cm) tall by 4 1/2" (11cm) wide at the bottom and 2" (5cm) wide at the top, from a sheet of metallic purple clay 3/16" (5mm) thick. Connect the pieces along one long edge to create the under-robe. Press with fabric for texture. Cut a 9" x 1/2" (23cm x 13mm) strip from a sheet of gold clay 1/16" (2mm) thick. Lay the gold along the bottom of the under-robe. Cut 1/4" (6mm) leaf shapes from a sheet of metallic green clay 1/16" (1mm) thick, using a leaf cutter. Press the leaves on top of the gold strip. If you don't have a leaf cutter, roll tiny, flattened teardrop shapes.

8 Place the under-robe on the figure, overlapping the pieces at the left side. Use a sharp needle tool to press in the waistline. Lay the sheath top and the pouch flap along the waistline. Add the belt over the flaps. Overlap the ends of the belt. Fold the sheath top and pouch flap over the belt, being sure to press firmly enough to secure both to the under-robe. Use the tip of a knife to cut a buttonhole in the pouch flap, then add a button-shaped piece of gold clay. Wrap the sword with the sheath, then press the sword firmly to the sheath top.

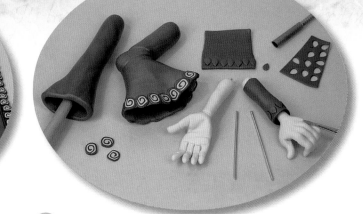

9 Cut two pieces, each 6¹/₂" (17cm) tall by 5" (13cm) wide at the bottom and 3" (8cm) wide at the top, from a sheet of metallic green clay flattened to ³/₁₆" (5mm) thick. Cut one piece in half lengthwise. Lay a half piece on either side of the larger piece to make a wide robe. Flatten the seams and bevel the edges, then add texture with fabric. To make a jelly roll design, lay a piece of purple and a piece of off-white clay, 2" x 3¹/₄" x ¹/₁₆" (5cm x 8cm x 2mm), on top of each other, then roll from a long side. Roll and stretch this jelly roll until it's ¹/₄" (6mm) in diameter. Cut thin slices of this jelly roll and press along the bottom and sides of the robe. Roll thin ropes from metallic blue clay, then press them along the row of jelly roll slices.

10 For arms, roll two 1¹/₄" (31mm) balls of metallic green clay into 3" (8cm) ropes. Use a blunt tool to hollow out the sleeves to the elbow. Bend the elbow over a tool, then add texture and wrinkle lines. Add slices of the jelly roll to the sleeve. Make hands, starting each with a ⁷/₈" (22mm) ball of flesh-colored clay rolled into a 2" (5cm) rope. The finished hands are 1¹/₃" (33mm) long. Insert a 1¹/₂" (4cm) rigid wire into each wrist to help support the hands. Wrap each wrist with a flattened purple strip embellished with leaf cutouts.

11 Press pleats and gathers into the top of the robe. Form soft folds along the robe. Set the figure on a piece of cardstock. Fit the robe around the neck and shoulders and make adjustments to the gathers and folds. Next, insert the hands into the sleeves and softly press the sleeves around the wrists. Drape excess clay to form wrinkles for realism. Press the sleeves in place at the shoulders, adding both sleeves at the same time. Position the staff in Drey's hand, using a brush as needed to close the fingers over the staff. Bake for 30 minutes, following the directions on the package of clay, then let the clay cool.

12 Press a flattened piece of off-white clay to the top of the head and around the chin. From a sheet of off-white clay ¹/₁₆" (1mm) thick, cut long, thin hair strips. Twist the strips, then, beginning at the bottom of the beard, attach by pressing them to the soft clay base. Add strands as needed to fill out the beard and hair. Use a knitting needle to hold and tuck in small pieces of hair. Add the mustache last. Brush liquid polymer clay along the hairline. Bake for at least 30 minutes, following the directions on the package of clay Let the clay cool. Apply a wash coat of watery brown paint to the face and hands. Add blush, then paint the eyes blue following the instructions on page 23.

wizard or king?

*d*rey Van Elm is one of those characters that can be dramatically altered with just a change of hats. He can easily perform the duties of the Elf King with a removable crown, but change his crown to a tall pointed hat and he becomes a wise wizard. If you make the hat and crown for Drey, bake them separately, then remove them from the oven while still hot and allow them to cool on Drey's head.

The crown

Cut a $^1/_2$" (13mm) wide strip that is long enough to fit around Drey's head from a sheet of gold clay $^1/_8$" (3mm) thick. Press a $1^1/_4$" (31mm), two $1^1/_8$" (28mm) and two $^3/_4$" (19mm) pieces of thin, rigid wire to the strip of clay. Shape leaves from flattened teardrops and add texture with a real leaf. Brush liquid polymer clay on the backs of the leaves, then press them over the wires, leaving the wire ends exposed. Press small metallic blue clay balls over the wire ends. Bake the crown, following the instructions on the package of clay, over a rolled piece of cardstock to keep the wires straight.

The wizard's hat

To make a tall wizard hat, flatten a $1^1/_4$" (31mm) metallic purple clay ball into a 3" (8cm) circle and cut out the center. Make the top from a $1^1/_4$" (31mm) ball of metallic purple clay that is rolled into a $2^1/_2$" (6cm) tall cone. Hollow out the cone with a blunt tool and turn under the edges. Set the cone on top of the circle and press the edges together. Add texture by pressing on the sides with a piece of cloth. Stretch the clay as needed so the hat is oversized. Bake the hat following the instructions on the package of clay.

Isa Rosalia
the garden fairy

ook, over there in the corner of the garden, under the daisies: Isa Rosalia, one of the Flower Fairies, is deep in thought. Perhaps she's heard the recent mumblings of the gnomes who say that she is arrogant and moody and quite a little princess (if you know what I mean).

I suspect that the problem is all about wings, and the fact that it takes a special kind of wisdom to be friends with someone who has gifts that we do not. Imagine having a friend with wings. Wings that can take her far away at a moment's notice, leaving you earth-bound and standing in the mud while she soars through sunbeams, over rainbows and beyond the stars.

No, it isn't easy in the Faerie world or in ours, to see beyond our own lives. But, oh, the lovely stories that we can share if we just make ourselves look past the wings.

One of the joys of making Faerie Folk is telling stories about their imagined lives. As we tell their stories, we listen, and we often hear our own world explained in ways that were never clear to us before. I invite you to tell more stories about Isa Rosalia and her friends. I want to know what happens next!

notes from Woodpecker Pete

Not to sound like a cantankerous old elf, but it is my experience that fairies tend to be temperamental, both in real life and in their clay versions. Their features, though beautiful, are small and refined, with very few character lines. This means that, if you don't want to offend any fairies, the sculpting has to be quite precise. What starts out to be a fairy can easily turn into a troll. If you are new at sculpting, you might consider enlarging the patterns to whatever size your oven will accommodate, so that you can work with larger features.

materials

Polymer clay: 3 ounces (85 grams) of violet, 1 ounce (28 grams) or less of copper, gold, leaf green, flesh color, translucent, ultramarine blue and white

Color recipes:
- For light ultramarine blue, mix 1 ounce (28 grams) of ultramarine with $^1/_4$ ounce (7 grams) of white
- For light violet, mix 3 ounces (85 grams) of violet with $^1/_2$ ounce (14 grams) of white
- For the eyes, use two prebaked $^1/_8$" (3mm) white clay balls

Matte liquid polymer clay

Two 8$^3/_4$" (22cm) and one 6$^1/_2$" (17cm) Soft Metal Rods (by AMACO)

8" (20cm) thin brass rod

Four 4" (10cm) pieces of 22-gauge wire

Four 4" (10cm) pieces of 28-gauge wire

White florist tape

Aluminum foil

Acrylic paints: brown, coral, blue, black and white

Matte medium or blending gel (for use with acrylic paints)

Denatured alcohol or clay softener

Instant glue

Imitation gold leaf

Furniture caster with toothed bottom (for use on rugs)

Drill

Paintbrush

Basic tools (page 12)

Patterns (page 125)

Isa Rosalia, as pictured, is 6$^1/_2$" (17cm) tall. Her head measures $^7/_8$" (2cm) from the bottom of her chin to the top of her head. This makes her almost 7$^1/_2$ heads tall.

115

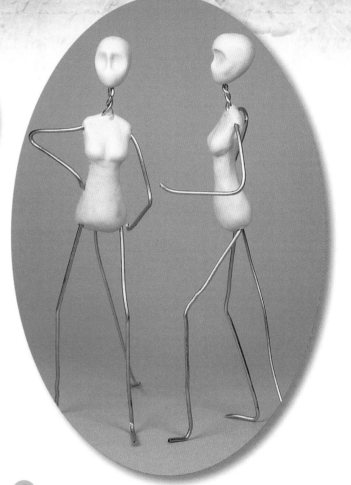

1 Use pliers to bend the 8³/₄" (22cm) brass rod, using the pattern on page 125 as a guide. Repeat with the second 8³/₄" (22cm) brass rod. Fold the 8" (20cm) thin brass wire in half. Twist the center of the wire several times to create a ⁵/₈" (16mm) loop and a long neck, following the pattern. Use pliers to bend the wire, using the trunk pattern as a guide. Lay all three wires on the body pattern, then wrap 28-gauge wires around the shoulders and hips to secure. The long wires become armatures for the leg and the opposite arm. Adjust and balance the armature so the character stands. Wad a flat piece of foil and insert it in the body. Wrap the body with foil, keeping the body thin. Tightly wrap the body (but not the neck) with florist tape. Bend a small loop at either end of the 6¹/₂" (17cm) wire. Position a loop against the back of the waist, then wrap it with 28-gauge wire to secure it. Wrap a small foil egg in the center of the head loop with foil, keeping the egg narrow. Make adjustments to the position of the body as needed.

2 Cover the body and head with a layer of flesh-colored clay ¹/₈" (3mm) thick. Shape the body by adding or carving away clay, as needed, to create a thin body and head. Add extra clay to form small breasts and buttocks. View the figure from all sides to be sure that it is graceful from every angle. Be careful not to add too much to the area where the head meets the neck, as the finished fairy will have a very long, thin neck. Bake the armature for 20 minutes in a preheated oven, following the directions on the package of clay.

3 To make legs, roll two ³/₄" (19mm) balls from flesh-colored clay. Roll each into a 3" (8cm) tapered rope. Slit the back of each leg from top to bottom. Press the split clay rope over a leg, pinching and compressing it to force out air and to shape the clay to the wire. Do this for both legs.

4 Blend and smooth the surface of each leg by smudging with a finger, then rolling with a needle tool. Stretching the clay as you blend will also help smooth the surface. Shape the knee. Bring the extra clay down to the foot. Shape a shoe with the toe turned up. Add and blend a tiny ball of clay onto each side of the ankle for an ankle bone. Brush or rub the surface with denatured alcohol or clay softener liquid for a final smoothing. The wires should still be visible at the tops of the legs so the legs can be repositioned. Prop the figure standing on the baking surface, and bake for 20 minutes. Let it cool.

notes

For this project, because the head is so small and the measurements at this size can be very imprecise, the shapes are listed rather than the exact dimensions. Make the pieces, try them on the figure to see if they fit, then adjust the sizes as needed.

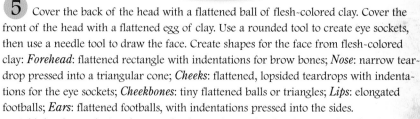

5 Cover the back of the head with a flattened ball of flesh-colored clay. Cover the front of the head with a flattened egg of clay. Use a rounded tool to create eye sockets, then use a needle tool to draw the face. Create shapes for the face from flesh-colored clay: *Forehead*: flattened rectangle with indentations for brow bones; *Nose*: narrow teardrop pressed into a triangular cone; *Cheeks*: flattened, lopsided teardrops with indentations for the eye sockets; *Cheekbones*: tiny flattened balls or triangles; *Lips*: elongated footballs; *Ears*: flattened footballs, with indentations pressed into the sides.

Add the shapes, laying them on the drawn face. Trim the pieces so the edges butt and don't overlap. Blend the seam lines. Shape and smooth the surface. Add the prebaked eyeballs, then add the eyelids.

6 View the face from all angles to check for symmetry. Add or trim away clay as needed. Press and blend the ears to the sides of the head. Stretch the tip of each ear to a point. Check the head again from all angles. Be sure that the area under the chin angles back toward the neck. Prop the figure in a standing position on the baking surface. Bake for 15 minutes, then let it cool.

7 Add clay to the arms just as you did to the legs, except start with a ⅝" (16mm) ball of clay this time. Add clay as needed to fill out the chest, neck, back and shoulders. Smooth and blend the clay. Add two thin ropes across the top of the chest for the collarbones and two more from the base of the neck to just behind the ears for the muscles.

8 Blend the seams so the collarbones and muscles are barely visible. Smooth areas that are hard to reach with a clay brush, then use a brush dipped in denatured alcohol or clay softener liquid for a final smoothing.

9 Make any necessary adjustments to the angle of the body and legs. Fill in the open area at the tops of the legs with light violet clay. Position the support wire so the fairy is stable and stands upright. Wrap the top of the support wire and hips with a light violet clay. Flatten the light violet clay to a sheet ⅛" (3mm) thick. Cut a petal shape 5" (13cm) long. Place the petal under the support wire. Fold the clay around the wire. Blend the petal into the clay at the hips. To make shoes, cut a strip of gold clay to fit under each foot. Pull up the edges to cover the heel and toe. Smooth and shape the shoes. Use a knife and a needle tool to gently trim away extra clay from the top of each foot.

10 Cut four 5" (13cm) tapered petals, seven 3½" (9cm) petals and three 2½" (6cm) petals from a sheet of violet clay. Curl and roll the petal ends, then press them to the waist. Press the tops around the hips, carving away any area that becomes too bulky. Be sure the waist remains thin. To make the top of the dress, cut a 1" x 2" (25mm x 5cm) strip from flattened sheet of gold clay. Roll two short gold ropes for straps.

12 For the hair, cut $1\,^1/_2$" (4cm) wide strips from a flattened sheet of copper clay. Cut the strips into a fringe. Pick up sections of the hair and separate the fringe with your fingers and twist the ends. Apply the hair, starting at the back of the head. Use shorter sections of hair for the bangs and sides. Position the strands in the back so the wings will fit between the shoulder blades. To make flowers, roll ten tiny white balls of clay for petals and three larger green balls for leaves. Roll each ball of clay into a teardrop shape, then flatten. Pick up the leaves, and then the petals, one at a time with a sharp needle tool, and press them in place. Prop the figure in a standing position on the baking surface and bake for 30 minutes. Let the clay cool.

11 Press the top of the dress on the figure, being careful not to damage the arms. Wrap the dress around the body and blend the seam in the back. Press the straps on the shoulders. Prop the figure in a standing position on the baking surface and bake for 20 minutes. Let it cool. Make $^5/_8$" (16mm) hands, starting with $^7/_{16}$" (11mm) balls of clay. Brush a small amount of matte liquid polymer clay on the ends of the arm wires. Press the hands in place and blend the seams of the arms. Be sure that the hands are securely attached. Use a brush and needle tool to shape the hand resting on the hip.

notes

If placing the dress top seems difficult without distressing the arms and chest area, you can bake the figure before adding the top, then bake the top when you bake the hair, after step 12. Use caution if your brand of clay scorches easily, as repeated baking may darken the nose and cheeks.

13 Antique the face with a very light coating of watery light brown paint. This should be just enough to define the creases. Dab blush made from a bit of coral paint mixed into matte medium or blending gel on the cheeks. Paint the eyes following the instructions on page 23. Add darker paint along the eyelids. The eyebrows and eyelashes are painted with light, lifting strokes using a nearly dry brush. Use a very tiny brush to add brown dots for freckles. These will help camouflage any imperfections in the surface that may have been caused by moisture or air bubbles in the clay.

14 To make the pattern for the wings, flatten light ultramarine blue, violet, gold and translucent clay to a sheet ¹/₈" (3mm) thick, or use the thickest setting on a pasta machine. Cut a 3" (8cm) square from each color. Stack the clay, with the translucent on the bottom and the blue on the top. Flatten the clay stack with a roller until the clay is ¹/₁₆" (2mm) thick. Cut the flattened stack in half, with the translucent layer on top. Apply a sheet of gold leaf to one half, then place the other half on top of the gold leaf, with the translucent side down.

15 Cut the layered stack in half again. Stack the halves together, this time with the blue on top. Set the stacked halves on a thick slab of gold clay. Press the clay firmly on the work surface so that it stays in place. Press the furniture caster into the stack of clay, then remove it. Use a very sharp clay blade to slice thin layers from the top of the clay slab. Use the wing pattern on page 125 to cut two large and two small wings from a sheet of translucent clay ¹/₁₆" (2mm) thick. Lay a 4" (10cm) piece of 22-gauge wire along one edge of each wing. Cover both sides of the wings with pieces of mokume gane patterned clay. Smooth the wings between your palms or between pieces of plain paper. Rip along the curved, bottom edge of the wing to create an interesting texture. Bake the wings for 30 minutes, following the directions on the package of clay. Let the clay cool.

16 Drill a single hole in the back of the fairy for the wings, being very careful not to drill through the figure. Begin with a very small hole, then enlarge it if necessary. Test to make sure that you are pleased with the angle of the wings and that the wires fit in the hole. Trim and adjust the wires if needed. Insert the wires in the hole, using instant glue to hold the wings in place.

sweet pea marie

Sweet Pea Marie likes upswept hair because it keeps her neck from sweating. Yes. Sweating. You may have thought that fairies, like princesses, never get nervous. But it takes a lot of work to look beautiful all the time. Upswept hair helps her appear regal and calm. Every girl has her secrets, even a fairy girl.

If you have trouble getting the skin on the fairy's arms or legs smooth, consider changing her outfit. To cover Sweet Pea Marie's shoulders and upper arms, short petal shapes, similar to those used for the skirt, were pressed over her shoulders, then baked at the same time as her hair.

The colors used to make Sweet Pea's clothing and wings are purple, gold, magenta and light beige. Mix small amounts of light beige into the colors to lighten them. Mix magenta and purple together to create an in-between color for some of the petals. Her hair is translucent, light beige and gold mixed together, then left slightly streaked.

Upswept hair

1 To make upswept hair, begin by pressing clay onto the head, ending it just above the hairline. Cut 1¹/₂" (4cm) long strips of hair and press them to the hairline with all the strands hanging down.

2 Lift a few strands up to the center of the head at a time. Press the ends together, then cut off the excess clay. Indent the hair with a needle tool to flatten and groom specific areas. Use a brush to lift or blend other areas. Make individual curls to fill in the sides, bangs and top. Press the hair in place with a knitting needle.

patterns

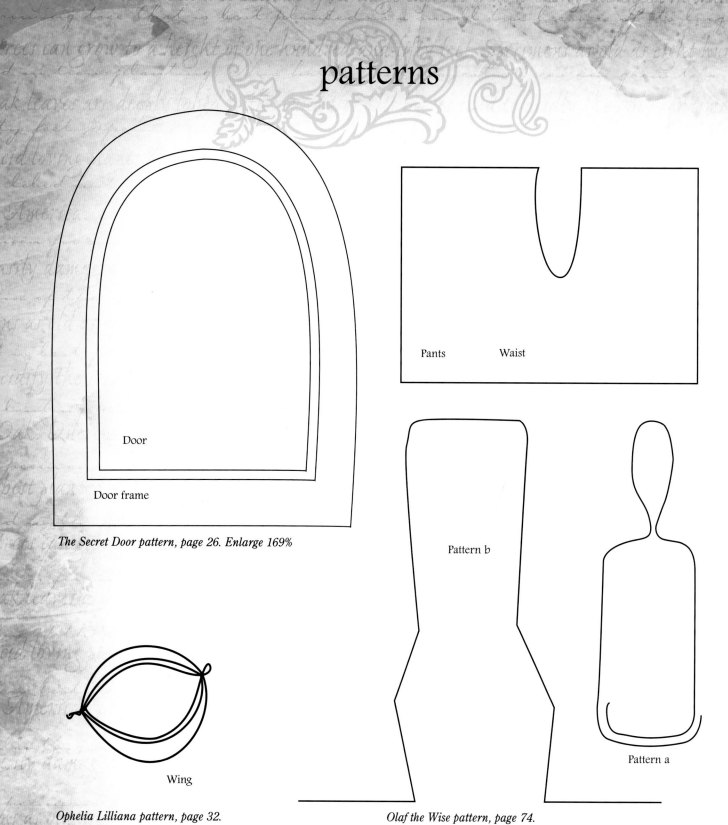

Door

Door frame

Pants   Waist

Pattern b

Pattern a

The Secret Door pattern, page 26. Enlarge 169%

Wing

Ophelia Lilliana pattern, page 32.

Olaf the Wise pattern, page 74.

patterns

AnnaBelle Mae pattern, page 82.

Shirt

Sleeve cap

Vest

Cuff

Skirt

patterns

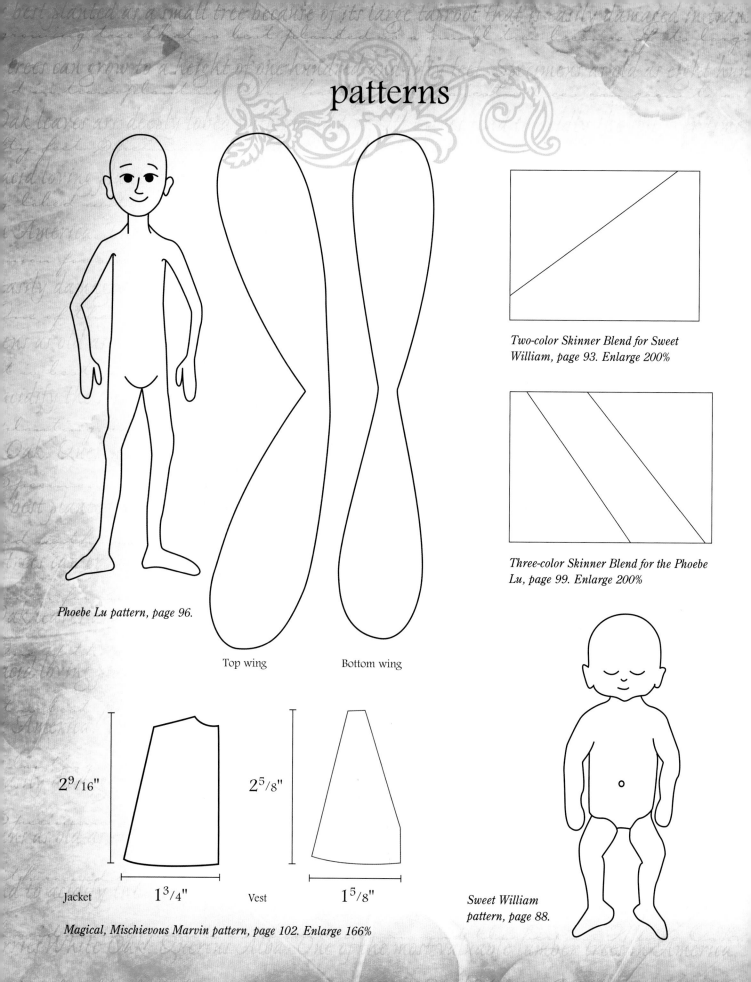

Phoebe Lu pattern, page 96.

Top wing

Bottom wing

Two-color Skinner Blend for Sweet William, page 93. Enlarge 200%

Three-color Skinner Blend for the Phoebe Lu, page 99. Enlarge 200%

$2^9/16$"

$2^5/8$"

Jacket $1^3/4$"

Vest $1^5/8$"

Magical, Mischievous Marvin pattern, page 102. Enlarge 166%

Sweet William pattern, page 88.

patterns

Isa Rosalia pattern, page 114.

Body outline

Body armature a

Body armature b

Wing a

Wing b

resources

polymer clay manufacturers and suppliers

American Art Clay Co., Inc. (AMACO)
Telephone: (800) 374-1600
Web site: www.amaco.com
Importer and distributor of FIMO Classic, FIMO Soft; manufacturer and/or distributor of gold leaf, WireForm, armature rods, clay blades, push molds, tools and polymer clay accessories

Kato Polyclay/Van Aken International
Telephone: (909) 980-2001
Web site: katopolyclay.com
Manufacturer of Kato Polyclay and Kato Polyclay Clear Medium; manufacturer and/or distributor of clay blades and tools.

Polyform Products
Telephone: (847) 427-0020
Web site: www.sculpey.com
Manufacturer of Premo! Sculpey plus other Sculpey labels; manufacturer and/or distributor of polymer clay tools.

organizations

Polymer clay guilds: There are polymer clay guilds in almost every part of the United States plus in many other countries. For information about these guilds and for links to various polymer clay related Web sites, see the National Polymer Clay Guild Web site at www.npcg.org.

Dollmaking: To see the work of some of the world's best dollmakers, including many who work with polymer clay, go to www.niada.org.

magazines

Two of my favorite magazines for both character inspiration and technical information are:

Art Doll Quarterly
(877) 782-6737 or www.artdollquarterly.com

Polymer Café Magazine
(800) 458-8237 or www.polymercafe.com

inspiration

Here is a short list of a few of the artists and authors who inspire me:

Artist, illustrator and author James Christensen

Polymer clay artist and author Katherine Dewey; see her work at www.elvenwork.com

Artist and author Brian Froud

Photographer and author of many books, Anne Geddes, whose calendars and journals feature babies and children in fantasy settings

Authors and illustrators Lauren Mills and Dennis Nolan

index

Take a Creative Journey
with North Light Books

Enchanted Garden Crafts
By Susan Cousineau

Inside this idea-packed project book, you'll find 25 quick-and-easy projects inspired by the natural beauty of the garden. From garden party crafts and Easter decorations to nature gifts and garden-themed keepsakes, *Enchanted by the Garden* gives you plenty of ways to celebrate the abundance of your garden. Many of the projects can be made in just a few steps, so they're easy for kids. The projects also include templates and use craft supplies that you already have at home. Get started now and fill your garden and your home with lovely decorations and keepsakes.

ISBN-10 1-58180-449-0
ISBN-13 978-1-58180-449-2
Paperback, 64 pages, 32697

Clay Characters for Kids
By Maureen Carlson

Create a world of fun and enchantment with polymer clay! You can transform a batch of colorful polymer clay into a fantasy world right out of your imagination. Children and beginners will find basic techniques for 10 easy shapes that can be used to create dozens of different creatures and characters, plus instruction for faces, eyes, noses, ears, mouths, hands, paws and feet. Learn how to create 30 detailed and colorful fantasy characters in all. Bring your imagination to life today!

ISBN-10 1-58180-286-2
ISBN-13 978-1-58180-286-3
paperback, 80 pages, 32161

Polymer Clay for the Fun of It!
By Kim Cavender

As every polymer person knows, working with polymer clay is all about having fun and making great stuff. With its over 20 bright and colorful projects and variations, *Polymer Clay for the Fun of It!* shows readers how to have a good time with polymer clay. The book gives readers a comprehensive and lighthearted polymer clay "primer" along with a detailed techniques section to make getting started fun and easy. As a bonus feature, readers get "Just for the fun of it..." tips to keep them inspired. Each project begins with an often tongue-in-cheek quote that matches the easygoing tone of the book. With *Polymer Clay for the Fun of It!* you can throw all of the rules out the window and just, well, have fun!

ISBN-10 1-58180-684-1
ISBN-13 978-1-58180-684-7
paperback, 128 pages, 33320

THESE AND OTHER FINE NORTH LIGHT TITLES ARE AVAILABLE FROM YOUR LOCAL ART AND CRAFT RETAILER, BOOKSTORE OR ONLINE SUPPLIER.